Preventing Exclusions

by
Adam Abdelnoor

Heinemann Educational Publishers
Halley Court, Jordan Hill, Oxford OX2 8EJ
A division of Reed Educational & Professional Publishing Ltd

OXFORD   MELBOURNE   AUCKLAND
JOHANNESBURG   BLANTYRE   GABORONE
IBADAN   PORTSMOUTH (NH) USA   CHICAGO

Heinemann is a registered trademark of Reed Educational & Professional
Publishing Ltd

First published 1999

03 02 01 00 99
10 9 8 7 6 5 4 3 2 1

British Library Cataloguing in Publication Data
A catalogue record for this book is available from the British Library.

ISBN 0 435 80039 6

Typeset and illustrated by 𝔸 Tek-Art, Croydon, Surrey
Printed and bound in Great Britain by Biddles Ltd, Guildford

Acknowledgements
The publishers have made every effort to contact copyright holders. However,
if any material has been incorrectly acknowledged, the publishers would be
pleased to correct this at the earliest opportunity.

Contents

Preface

In setting out to write a book about reducing school exclusions, an attempt must be made to integrate the many, fragmented and apparently irreconcilable perspectives on difficult children – from the pupils' own disjointed and confused outlook, through parental 'third party' involvement and teachers' and professionals' narrower but decisive opinions, to managerial concerns. Overall, there is a lack of clarity about how to view the issue.

Schools and authorities would do well to recognise the value of placing behavioural difficulties squarely within a special-needs framework, avoiding the false dichotomy between these difficulties and those of learning. It is a false dichotomy because we know that, regardless of which came first and how they are related, behavioural difficulties go hand in hand with learning deficits. To recognise this means that we have a ready-made code to apply to difficult children and this, together with the new guidance on exclusions to which the Department for Education and Employment has given limited statutory force, will provide downward pressure on the frequency of exclusions.

That wholesale reductions are possible is borne out by the differences between exclusion rates in different countries in the UK. The rate is highest in England, where the frequency of exclusions is nine times higher than in Northern Ireland, four times higher than in Scotland, and 60 per cent higher than in Wales. In Scotland exclusions are the responsibility of the local authority, not the school, and some authorities do not allow permanent exclusion – there were no permanent exclusions in Glasgow in 1996/97. When permanent exclusion is being considered in Northern Ireland, the future education of the excludee must be planned out, and this is perhaps one of the main reasons why exclusion rates there are low. In Europe, too, head teachers have a responsibility to find alternative schooling, if they want to require a pupil to leave their school.

Pupils with learning difficulties may be given learning support amounting to around one day per week for periods of about a year, which can be extended at the annual review. This kind of regular and curriculum-related support is less effective when applied to behavioural needs, because behavioural difficulties are much more unpredictable than learning difficulties and have a very different impact on the social environment in which they occur.

In-class learning support will have a clearly defined function and *modus operandi* often focusing on a particular subject. Problem pupils require a different kind of support, which is sporadic but recurring, sometimes in-school and sometimes out-of-school, and may consist of brief bursts or substantial intervention, followed by a brief course of therapy, then occasional monitoring, and good liaison with parents which may enable problems to be picked up in advance. There might be gaps during which nothing is done and then, at times of stress, a need for more intervention. Funding issues will continue to be at the forefront in discussions of development in this area.

In the vast majority of cases, exclusion is not the only option – but finding better solutions is a real challenge. It requires a flexible approach and a willingness to be innovative. The term 'culture' is used throughout this book to mean a school's ethos, history and constitution, its catchment area, and racial, religious and ethnic mix, as well as most aspects of its functioning including its infrastructure, staff and staffing structure, procedural framework, governance and educational approach. Culture here is the soil in which the pupils are the growing shoots. This book will show how the culture of a school can evolve to embrace *all* pupils, especially those who become marginalised (for reasons which sometimes seem inexplicable). This is what is meant by *inclusion*.

The story of Jacob – and why this book was written

Jacob came from a North East African refugee one-parent family, and was in his final year at secondary school and expecting to take his GCSEs. An assessment was needed in order to decide whether to uphold his appeal against permanent exclusion. I saw him with his mother, sister and brother for two hours late on a Thursday evening at their fourth-floor flat on a large council estate, and they showed me the exclusion report and accompanying documentation.

Jacob was a complex pupil who had a social–relational disability characterised by difficulties in relating to others, and in understanding and construing social situations. I was not at all surprised that he should get into trouble, behave inappropriately and then naively try to cover things up with half-truths and feeble excuses. His efforts to win peer approval were likely to be misguided and ineffective.

He admitted to being sad and often lonely. Many of his friends had left the previous year. His mother understood him well, and sometimes allowed him not to attend school. She said that she had wanted help for him, and had tried to get it from a very early age. Although several educational psychologists had apparently agreed that he had special needs, there had been very little in the way of therapeutic intervention. As his mother explained:

They come and they talk to us, and ask Jacob questions and then they go and we never see them again.

This was a pupil who had been allowed to 'slip through the cracks'. We (by which I mean the community) had a moral obligation to try to help him and his family. When asked if he thought he could get his GCSEs, if he worked as hard as he could and all the other problems were removed, Jacob shook his head sadly. His learning deficits were a heavy load for him to carry.

Jacob had learning, emotional and behavioural problems. However, if he had been happy in himself and could work at a suitable level, he would probably behave – he was still very dependent on his mother,

1

and wanted to please her. The absence of any determined and focused attempt to address his special needs over many years, and the failure to recognise his social–relational disability (akin to mild autism), had become part of the problem.

He and his family were very upset about the permanent exclusion, and the fact that the very negative report did not acknowledge that the system had let him down. This rejection, so close to the end of his compulsory schooling, could be seen as harsh. There were compassionate grounds for a positive response to their strongly expressed desire for him to stay at school for the two remaining terms, without the stain of permanent exclusion on his character.

Jacob and his family were desperate for help. In order for a return to school to have had any hope of success, his learning, emotional and behavioural needs would have had to be addressed, and teachers in the school would have had to be willing to accept Jacob back, and be aware that he had a 'special' kind of problem.

Jacob would have needed realistic achievement targets, and a reduction in the number of GCSEs he was to take to perhaps three or four. He also needed a period of intensive learning support preferably delivered on a one-to-one basis. His sister and mother could have assisted in the completion of extra learning tasks, especially non-verbal and verbal reasoning tests at an appropriate level. He needed regular one-to-one sessions to help him understand himself better and develop a more positive outlook on life. In particular, he needed to begin to accept himself and his limitations. On returning he would have continued to need special education support provided by teachers, and extra pastoral support because of his unusually high anxiety level. He would have continued to show this anxiety – implicitly by his behaviour. Jacob could also have been enrolled in the local 'befriender' scheme. Over a period of time, he would have become more confident, relaxed and cheerful, but this could not be achieved overnight.

Although his behaviour problems were high on most teachers' lists of concerns, in this case they were not the crucial issue. If Jacob could have coped with the academic expectations, and had had help with his social problems, his behaviour would probably have improved of itself. But these improvements would have taken some time to become apparent and the school would have needed to work out a fairly sophisticated strategy for balancing his time in class and time spent out of class having personal tuition or mentoring (especially in the early stages). So empathy and acceptance from staff would have been essential.

What are we to make of the self-evident opposition of some staff to providing this level of flexible, sensitive support? Traditionalists might view school as a place of learning in which teachers (all powerful) provide education (academic) to students (obedient). This perspective has its enchanting qualities, but one major drawback – it is outmoded and dysfunctional. Students need more than academic development. The contemporary culture is creating a more complex, exciting, and chaotic lifestyle than was dreamed of in the postwar years. The expectations are higher, the outlook more sophisticated and there is an awareness of adulthood and individual rights which represents freedom and pain to the emergent young adult. We have a duty to those who are unable to cope, and show this by their stressed and stressful behaviour.

In the end, the governors felt they could not reverse, on appeal, the decision to permanently exclude. Having seen the tears of his mother, his sister and of Jacob himself, I am in no doubt as to the grief this caused. It was transparently obvious that Jacob (and his mother) had poor social skills, and had needed help right from the start. Why could our system not have provided it?

1 Inclusion from the beginning

▰ The importance of 'relationship'

In considering the problem of children who are at risk of school failure, one observation seems more relevant than any other: teachers teach, and pupils learn, in the context of social relationships. It is remarkable that the vast majority of relationships in a school are functional enough to allow the process of education to carry on. When relationships become dysfunctional, efforts to repair them should focus on improving communication, encouraging those concerned to share their different views, and the search for acceptable compromises with which all those involved can live.

Not every relationship can be saved, but where those involved are prepared to try, success is much more likely. In an educational context, 'all those concerned' means pupils, teachers and family. Young people are not very good at keeping their home lives and their working lives separate, and so family relationships are important to educational success. The approach advocated in this book reflects the importance of 'relationship' in turning the risk of failure into the chance of success, and in doing so implicitly recognises that 'I can't change unless you do, and you can't change unless I do'. This means working to produce real partnership between staff and pupils.

Key objectives of the book are to accurately describe excluded pupils, to identify common axes underlying their situations, to outline an approach to the management of their needs and the reversal of the downward spiral, and to consider the wider perspective in terms of implementation and policy development. This book describes various types of excludees and their families, advances some views based on working experience as to the core processes underlying exclusion, and describes and assesses an approach to successful reintegration for the groups of pupils for whom – on the basis of justifiable criteria – this is an appropriate option.

▓ Reintegration

The word 'reintegration' requires a special definition for this book. It is used to describe the process of moving a pupil from the margins to the heart of the school, as well as for bringing excluded pupils on to roll.

Pupils who are receiving fixed-term exclusions are much more likely to become, in due course, permanently excluded. Therefore, the use of the term 'reintegration' to describe their diversion from this course is prospectively timely. Most pupils go through crises at some stage in their education, and periods when things are 'not OK'. So one difficulty has been to decide how grave the concerns need to be before strategies going beyond the school boundary become advisable. Pupils who are permanently excluded usually spend some time hovering on the margins academically, behaviourally, emotionally and socially.

Who has responsibility for managing and co-ordinating the necessary interventions which pupils in difficulty may need? This is a key question for senior managers. Can they do it themselves? If someone is needed to provide outreach, how will this be resourced? If outside agencies are to do this, what are the factors on which success depends? This book explores the answers to these questions, but it should be borne in mind that senior managers need to stay, and be seen to stay, in control of these intervention processes if at all possible.

We need to be quite clear what is meant by 'intervention', and who does it. In a wider sense, every action by any teacher in response to the behaviour of pupils, which is not part of the specific process of their education, is an intervention. In this sense, telling a pupil to 'hurry up and get to class', or 'stop talking', or 'go and see Mr Jones after break' is an intervention. But this book is not about managing the day-to-day problems of the ordinary pupil, for which each school should have a whole-school behaviour-management system applied by teachers who should have a basic professional competence. It is about working with children who are at risk of school failure – those for whom there is a special anxiety, who come with a record of sometimes serious, incidents.

In the context of this book, an intervention consists of a cluster of more or less systematic strategies which have been chosen as being most likely to divert a pupil away from school failure, culminating in fixed-term or permanent exclusion. Interventions can be implemented by a number of people including staff, parents, other pupils or professionals, or even the pupil who is at risk.

▉ The social context

Schools are institutions established by the community to serve the community. To paraphrase John Donne, 'no school is an island'. Senior managers and governors are responsible for children in their own locality, and have a role to play in community development over decades. The cycle of antisocial behaviour and social alienation runs through the school culture. The opportunity to effect real change lies within the decision-making processes of this culture.

'Exclusion' is a term which in the wider social context can have little meaning. Pupils after all can only be moved from one part of the community to another. The only way to exclude a pupil permanently from the community would be by summary execution! This is more than a semantic distinction. Excluded children come to the attention of other educational institutions, welfare officers, social workers, the youth justice system and so on, with all the additional baggage and the labels which go with it. Distanced from a pupil's history, the receiving professionals are obliged to work from one-sided reports to understand and relate to the child whose pain is frequently concealed within a tough exterior. In the excluding school, other pupils take their place in the role of 'bad-boy', 'rude-boy' or, as teachers term it, the 'focus of disaffection' in the group.

Under sections 11 and 12 of the Education Act 1997 any pupil excluded twice, like Nathan (see Appendix 1), would lose his or her entitlement to a place in any school, where one would be available to a similar pupil without such an exclusion history. Surely, this is a retrograde step in the development of a caring society. What hope can such a pupil, or his family, have?

Partnership is currently one of the buzz-words in social and community management. It is an important value. School failure is a partnership too: schools, pupils, families and peer groups all contribute to a greater or lesser extent. Pupils themselves have contributed to the problem, and beyond the school's horizon families and peer group too. But schools should feel themselves strong enough to accept criticism where they have failed to meet the needs of individual pupils.

Despite the views of some politically motivated organisations, there is a clear social value resulting from an inclusive ideology, and a commitment to the mainstream is in everyone's interests. 'Special education' is notoriously expensive and the cost extends over the long term. Excluded pupils themselves become parents of excluded children, thus perpetuating the cost for the next generation. Excluded pupils are more likely to get into trouble in young adulthood, and there is a collateral pattern in the causes of delinquency and criminal behaviour, and factors underlying exclusion which would suggest that efforts to remedy the out-of-school causes of in-school problem behaviour would have a long-term beneficial effect, as indicated by behaviour in later life, and the behaviour of progeny. There are obvious and well-rehearsed strategic difficulties in proving social effects over decades, but the methodological problems of demonstrating quantitatively that remedial programmes 'work' should not be allowed to detract from their value as evidenced by qualitative methods.

▇ Social deprivation

It may be tempting to blame the catchment area for high levels of disruptive behaviour and exclusion, but this is not borne out by the evidence. Schools can overcome the social disadvantage of the pupils and families they serve by creating a positive ethos which encourages self-belief in pupils – and staff.

A frequently espoused cause of school failure is social deprivation. Although measures do exist that are designed to quantify social deprivation, the concept is very difficult to apply 'on the ground'. It is a catch-all term which may be useful for spotting trends and planning policy, but it often comes to be used as synonymous with low income, poverty or poor housing. Although these factors are interlinked, they are not the same. The use of the term 'social deprivation' obscures the diversity of interactions which lead to permanent exclusion and implies that in some ill-defined way 'poverty' (as the term is often taken to mean) is the cause of exclusion. But fewer than 1 per cent of pupils are permanently excluded (Parsons, 1999) although poverty, however defined, is far more widespread.

Social deprivation is difficult to define properly at all in a way that lends itself to functional operations such as intervention for excluded children. It creates the impression of being a relatively stable condition about which very little can be done in the short term. The view that it is a root cause of permanent exclusion denigrates the poor and reflects patronising middle-class attitudes. It can also become an excuse for inaction and belongs on the political agendas of those who would rather use excluded pupils as pawns in the game than take the relatively inexpensive steps required to support their reintegration.

Finally, whilst it may be true that social hardship is frequently a factor in the family life of pupils who have problems in school, it does not lend itself to the structured management of change advocated earlier in this chapter. What is needed is the inside perspective on the social needs of the family. Parents are unlikely to say 'I am socially deprived'. They may talk about the difficulties of finding a nursery place for their youngest child, and other childcare problems. These are the authentic issues, and they may well be soluble.

In conclusion, whilst the construct 'social deprivation' may be useful for some purposes, it is much more useful to talk about individual needs in a specific context. Of course 'security of attachment' and parenting are of huge importance. But (as one of many such examples) Rod Steiger never knew his father, and his mother was an alcoholic. He had only one year of high-school education. Why is he a successful actor now, and not languishing in a penitentiary somewhere in the American Deep South? Some researchers (e.g. Rutter, 1979) want to create a secondary construct which they call 'hardiness' and argue that the Steigers of this world are hardy, whereas the failures are not. My view is that the real explanation lies in the subtle differences between their life experiences or in other words, in the 'fine print' rather than the 'headline'.

▓ Style, strategy and structure within the school setting

The approach advocated in this book operates on three levels. *Style is important!* It is easy to forget that school pupils are children – as such, they may be immature, oversensitive or reckless. Their emotions can cloud their judgment to an extraordinary degree, and their ability to think systematically is still developing. Their outlook can change from hour to hour, and although they can be obstinate and obtuse, they can also change impulsively. Pupils who are at risk of school failure frequently come from families where parents are also struggling. Parents may be insecure, over-anxious, hostile or resentful of authority. They often carry unhelpful baggage from their own schooldays, and may be defensive or resistant to the efforts of professionals to become involved, however positively, in their lives. They may need help to build the social skills needed to make a constructive relationship with the school. However, there is a danger of stereotyping parents, who may instead seem well-adjusted, and perplexed by their children's problems.

For all these reasons, pupils and their parents are likely to conceal truths from professionals, whether they be school, staff or others who have become involved. This concealment puts the professional at a distinct disadvantage. The first task, then, is to build trust, mutual confidence and understanding. This book describes how it can be done. This is what is meant by 'style'. Whatever the level of intervention, style is important.

When it comes to teachers, all pupils have their favourites and their pet hates. It is somewhat chastening to realise how high the consensus view between different children can be. These views frequently depend on whether the teacher is seen as a fair, but firm person with a sense of humour, who likes the pupils. The style of each individual teacher is of crucial importance. Some of them seem to be able to work with the most difficult children, and if asked they often comment on positive aspects of a particular child, to which the teachers having more difficulties are completely blind. Mutual respect, mutual affection and mutual tolerance are communicated by style. Which of these statements is more likely to obtain a pupil's co-operation?

'Sit down.'
'John, if you don't sit down now I'm going to come and sit on you!'

Curiously, the first one is much more confrontational because it contains no affection. However nicely it is said, it remains a command. The second one, involving an unlikely and amusing threat, using the pupil's name, and said affectionately, will elicit co-operation with a teacher who has already established rapport and knows how and when to smile. Furthermore, this same teacher is likely to make the time to talk quietly on a one-to-one basis with John, and try to facilitate a more positive attitude from him, too. A few years ago I worked with a marvellous teacher in a school for children with moderate learning difficulties. She was embarrassingly politically incorrect, and phrases like 'you stupid idiot' and 'don't be such a numbskull' were frequently used. But she loved the pupils and they loved her, and she also praised them to the heavens for their achievements. As a result, her Year 11 class worked hard, did not drop out (as so often happens in the leaver's year), and learned a very important distinction, aptly summed up by one of her pupils when she said 'I may be thick but I'm not stupid!' Such self-respect does not come easily to people who go to a special school. Style is important, backed up by finer human qualities.

Some pupils have problems which seem to self-extinguish, or which are amenable to the whole-school behaviour-management policy. The behaviour of others more or less rapidly deteriorates.

The appropriate strategy or strategies to be used will depend on the number and severity of the problems the assessment has uncovered. There are a wide range of strategies that might be employed and this book describes many, but certainly not all, of them. The same strategies might be utilised for a pupil who has only recently become 'a problem' and one who has been permanently excluded from one school and is trying to return to another. Pupils in the latter group were in the former group a little while ago!

The perspicacity and experience of senior managers will be an important factor in how decisions are made about the severity of a particular case, and the best way forward.

Very often, pupils who are permanently excluded midway through their secondary schooling had problems in primary school. Unfortunately, hindsight is no help to current decision-making (and as with 'social deprivation' the lack of early intervention should not be used as an excuse for saying 'it's too late now'). Like the police, who cannot arrest someone simply because they are likely to commit a crime, school managers cannot use up precious special needs without good reason, when there is such a demand for them. Early intervention is therefore important and worth developing, but it is not a sinecure for all children at risk of failure. The guidance from the Department for Education and Employment (DfEE, 1999) offers a useful case study of a primary school in which disruptive children have some special provision. But what about problems associated with adolescence, or those which are manageable in the primary phase, and will either self-extinguish or become much less manageable at secondary phase? In short, primary schools should not turn a blind eye to emergent special needs, but cannot be expected to act pre-emptively over feelings of disquiet, or label all naughty little children as having special needs.

Decisions about what strategies should be implemented in a particular case will depend on a careful assessment of the pupil at school, at home and as an individual. However, obtaining a really comprehensive assessment is itself a lengthy process involving resources from outside the school, and so it is likely that only those pupils who are on the very edge of a complete breakdown in their schooling will be offered this opportunity.

Government money is now being made available (chiefly through the Standards Fund) to enable schools and authorities to take more proactive steps to intervene effectively, and so the funds to pay for the strategies suggested in this book may now become accessible to more schools.

Any strategic individual plan must operate within a *structure*. For instance, whilst the reasons behind a pupil's permanent exclusion may not have changed, the context in which action can be taken will have shifted from one school to another educational setting – hopefully another mainstream school. Furthermore, the professionals to whom the pupil is referred will operate from a variety of different agencies. This may be Educational Welfare, Educational Psychology, the school's own Special Educational Needs (SEN) department, a specialised local service, a Pupil Referral Unit (PRU), and so on. How resources are accessed will depend on the local infrastructure – many schools have home–school liaison teams, or outreach workers for particular ethnic or racial groups. Structure is considered in more detail later in the book.

■ Race and ethnicity

The question of bias in exclusion rates for some ethnic minority children is sufficiently important to merit a separate section here. The issue is discussed later under 'demographics', 'the Macpherson report', 'equal opportunities' and 'elective exclusion'. We know that, proportionately, more than six times as many African–Caribbean children as white UK children are excluded. This sounds prejudicial. However, ten times as many children in care are excluded as those living at home, and many of these are white. We also know that four times as many English pupils are excluded from English schools as Scottish children from Scottish schools, although there are apparently no differences between exclusions of Scottish and English children in English schools. In short, simple explanations will not suffice.

It has been suggested that the ethnic differences in exclusion rates 'cannot be merely teacher prejudice', but must be something to do with peer-group cultures. Well, if this is partly true in a sense, it is also a highly political statement. I have pointed out elsewhere that statements like 'social deprivation is a cause of school exclusion' and 'there needs to be more early intervention' can both be used politically to offset responsibility for dealing constructively with current problems. (Another well-used argument is 'teachers must have the right to exclude children, to protect themselves from violent attacks', but fewer than one permanent exclusion in 80 is the result of violence towards teachers.) The assertion that 'the different African–Caribbean culture explains why African–Caribbean children get excluded more often' is harder to disprove because it is so vague, and far more damaging.

First let's ensure that:

■ unwitting prejudice, ignorance and fear is completely displaced from our schools (if you are in any doubt about unwitting prejudice, three real-life examples are given later in the book – see 'Macpherson');

■ we get to grips with the way a predominant culture (e.g. white UK) impacts on the values and effectiveness of a minority culture (whether it be African–Caribbean, Arab or other), especially the underlying issues of power, control, and identity;

and *then* we can look at how developments in African–Caribbean culture may contribute to the solution. Every child is different, and many cultural issues are actually family issues, and only partially related to culture.

Having said all this, it is now safe to say that we need to understand ethnic family life and culture from its own perspective. To do so will involve mutual dialogue with representatives of that culture, and in the process both sides will discover ways in which change can occur. It really is too early at this stage to apportion responsibility.

One area which must be worth further examination is the gender differences within different cultures. In some cultures boys do as well as girls but in others far worse. Arab girls do as well as Arab boys for instance, but African–Caribbean boys do worse than their sisters. Inasmuch as the cultural background of the two is similar (one cannot say the same, since girls fare very differently in a family setting) this suggests something *intracultural* rather than *intercultural*. There may be a starting off point here.

▓ Individual needs

Excluded children are not a homogeneous group, and exclusion is more of a socially induced condition than a mental health problem. Emotional damage, family problems, educational shortcomings and the inevitable alienation following exclusion create a comprehensively discouraging scenario for the average excludee. Nevertheless, in addressing the needs of excluded children the concept of 'therapy' or 'treatment' is an appropriate one, partly because the pupil (and family) start to believe there really is something constitutionally wrong with them.

The presenting problems may be educational, but the underlying causes frequently depend on domestic and personal circumstances, and the individual's psychology, and so the remedies frequently lie outside school. The approaches adopted when working with excluded children are different from a school-based programme, so a different kind of thinking must prevail. The needs of the excluded child and his or her family are independent of the uniform and regular structures of day-to-day school life. Where in-school programmes for dealing with pupils at risk of failure have worked there is no need for continuing exclusion. But if it has proved necessary, then in-school programmes are obviously not adequate. However, for the moment, school managers are responsible for the reintegration of their own problem children, and frequently for the problem children which another school has off-loaded. Hence the need for this book.

Permanently excluded children have suffered a momentous traumatic rejection by their community. The psychosocial vulnerabilities which invariably underlie their alienation have been manifested, and the social systems designed to address this are still developing. Parents and families whose inadequacies are often a factor in exclusion are placed under still greater strain and need help to cope, although their experience is one of rejection and condemnation. The conditions which led to exclusion have frequently already undermined academic progress to the extent that substantial learning deficits have built up. These factors are interdependent and cause and affect are very difficult to distinguish satisfactorily.

Without assistance, the route back into mainstream education (if it is attempted at all) will usually be tortuous and stressful. Schools and teachers routinely re-enact the process of rejection when the pupils reaffirm their sense of failure by repeating the behaviour leading to exclusion. Staff are reluctant to accept these 'pariahs', and will sometimes even attempt to sabotage placements.

The social psychology of the exclusion itself, the excludee's psychosocial needs, family (dys)function, and the dynamics of the receiving institution, form an 'ecosystem', the whole of which must be taken into account when managing reintegration.

Furthermore, a small proportion of excluded children are not suitable for mainstream reintegration, but there is as yet no truly reliable means of assessing this. It also depends on the school, the teachers and the effectiveness of interventions. It may seem as if there is a great deal, even too much, emphasis placed on how professionals are behaving, and not enough on the pupil's own behaviour. This could be seen as unconstructive criticism of staff (which it is not meant to be) or an affirmation of how powerful staff, in reality, are. To use that power effectively they need to understand what is wrong, taking into account what is happening outside school, and have the skills necessary to impact on the ecosystem.

▨ The multimodal approach

A multimodal approach incorporates a number of more specifically structured programmes (such as a suitably modified non-attendance programme) to provide a comprehensive intervention. Any programme of support and remediation needs to be practical, and process- or outcome-led, rather than theory-generated. Any programme must be cost-effective and feasible in terms of resourcing, especially as regards personnel and training requirements. This book describes a successful approach to achieving mainstream reintegration following exclusion. It is equally applicable to the prevention of permanent exclusion, and reintegration following permanent exclusion. Although the same approach can be applied before or after resorting to a permanent solution, the latter group present the harder cases because of the emotional and social damage which results from permanent exclusion.

All this adds up to a programme which can take account of 'the social psychology' of exclusion.

- The accumulated 'rubbish' of school failure down the generations must be overcome. Parents of excluded children frequently had difficulties in school themselves. Sometimes, their school phobia is still intact and they find it hard to come on to a school site without feeling anxious and even confrontational. They are unable to show their children how to cope with school, and may even model or describe negative coping styles.

- The pupil projects a negative self-image on to the school system. Fear of academic inadequacy is rationalised as a belief that 'school is a waste of time', or 'the teachers wouldn't help me/picked on me when I asked for help'.

- Difficulties coping with stress overload lead to phantom sicknesses or staged conflicts which result in withdrawal. The pupil feels rejected, and the parents feel vindicated in their belief that they and their children are being victimised.

- Their child becomes a pariah, justifying the secret and unspeakable attitudes of some professionals, and the institutional closing of ranks.

Any programme which seeks to overcome this must first acknowledge and understand it.

There is a power imbalance between schools and pupils, which is just a reflection of the need for firm discipline and clear management in school. However, this does mean that children get lost in the system sometimes. So this book advocates strongly for the child's perspective. This does not mean teachers or schools are 'to blame'. Excluded children are victims of 'the system', but we are all victims of the system – and we all benefit from it. The machine of civilisation is something which just grinds on. This book is an attempt to be heard above its noise, and the message which staff need to hear is this: *Children at risk of failure in school can often be helped if communications are improved, all those concerned are facilitated to share their different views, and pupils get help to rebuild damaged relationships at home and at school. School staff and parents have a major role to play in achieving this.*

The monster theory

Excluded pupils are not monsters, as some organisations would like to portray them. Difficult behaviour in class is a real problem, and disruption, verbal and physical abuse are not tolerable. However, as

Warnock (1978) pointed out, the most stressful aspect of teaching is not the occasional critical incident but the chronic difficulties faced by teachers (particularly those who are inexperienced or ineffective) in schools with a high proportion of troublesome pupils. The stress of the unremitting, diffuse and intractable problems posed in class by the many, may create a professional state of mind in which the few become scapegoats – those whose behaviour is sufficiently serious to present a 'target'.

The excluded children I have worked with are *not* monsters. They are generally sad and dispirited, often deeply hurt and uncomprehending, and their misdemeanours seldom constituted a real crime in the legal sense, although they have been subjected to a quasi-legal process outside the accepted processes of jurisprudence. For most, as I shall show, simple and effective solutions could be found to expedite their reintegration back into the heart of the school. In many cases, these solutions could be applied more effectively before exclusion became necessary.

2 Developing relevant policies for marginalised children

▇ Demographics

Accurate figures for comparative purposes of the number of excluded children are now published for each LEA, though not yet for each school. Reasons for exclusions and longer term outcomes are less accurate – government figures (SEU, 1998) are based on a comprehensive survey (Parsons, 1995). It is difficult to accurately describe a situation which is constantly changing. About 25,000 children are not in school at any one time – mostly because of exclusion (SEU estimated). Exclusion rates for 1998 vary from 3.7 per 1,000 to 0.2 per 1,000. Many authorities recorded no exclusions of primary children, and on average the rate was less than one in 3,000. However, exclusions at primary ages have been rising (by 18% in 1995–6).

Rates peaked at around 13,600 in 1997 and have since dropped by a tiny amount (about 3%) – this has been described as a 'glimmer of hope' by one commentator. Full details of rates are published on the Internet (e.g. www.inaura.net/exclrate.htm). Comparisons between exclusion rates and GCSE scores (www.inaura.net/research) suggest that as exclusion rates drop, GCSE pass rates go up. Does this undermine the argument that academic achievement will be badly affected if schools are not allowed to exclude students? In fact, it is more likely that *schools that manage education better, also manage behaviour better*. This works across LEAs, too. Newham achieved the same GCSE pass rate as Westminster but permanent exclusion rates are one third there. 80% of Newham secondary school also earned a progress measure 'tick' in the GCSE league tables for 1998, so what is Newham doing right, *as an LEA*, that others might emulate?

In numerical terms, most excluded pupils are white, male, young teenagers. Eighty-three per cent of excluded pupils are boys, and 80 per cent are aged between 12 and 15 (half are 14 or 15). However, exclusion rates for children with special needs are six times higher than average, for African–Caribbean children they are more than six times higher; and for children in care they are ten times higher. Sixteen per cent of permanently excluded children are of ethnic minority origin; and nearly half of those are African–Caribbean. Yet African–Caribbean children make up only a little over 1 per cent of the school population.

One study (Graham, 1988) indicated that African–Caribbean children:

- were more likely to live with a lone parent;

- were more likely to be of above-average ability;

- were more likely to have been disruptive in primary and nursery schools;

- were less likely to show 'deep-seated trauma'.

It seems that early intervention, better understanding of the child-rearing difficulties faced by black single mothers, and understanding of how best to work with African–Caribbean children, could reduce the exclusion rate for this group. The need for this is underlined by an Office for Standards in Education (OfSTED) research study which suggested that tension and conflict between white teachers and African–Caribbean pupils resulted in more frequent complaints about 'troublesome' black pupils, high levels of criticism, excessive attempts to control black pupils, negative stereotyping, and the promotion by (and in) both pupils and teachers of a low-expectation low-ability, disruptive behaviour syndrome (Gillborn and Gipps, 1996).

Schools have to report fixed-term exclusions (defined as exclusions of between five and a maximum 45 days per term) to local education authorities, but the information is not centrally collated, although the DfEE plan to do so. OfSTED estimates that there are around 100,000 a year, but some of these may be repeat exclusions of the same child. All of these figures cover only decisions to exclude in any given year; they do not include children who were excluded in previous years and are still not in school. Anecdotal evidence suggests that children are sometimes excluded 'informally': one South London head teacher regularly tells pupils whom he wants to exclude:

> *You can't come back here, but I'll give you a few weeks to find another school, otherwise I will have to permanently exclude you – and you know what that means, don't you – the Shabby centre!*

The Shabby centre is the notoriously disorganised, oversubscribed and ineffective local PRU. When challenged by a support teacher he said: 'I know it's illegal.' His actions are an attempt to massage exclusion rates for his school, although the strategy often fails because other schools in the area want to know why the pupil is leaving. There are also likely to be many pupils who are officially on roll but whose attendance is very occasional. By a variety of artifices their absences fail to trigger a formal response (Still, 1989). Sometimes, for instance, unofficial exclusion is disguised as a medical problem (Stirling, 1992).

No more than a third of children who are permanently excluded are ever reintegrated back into school, mostly via the educational welfare service or via PRU/home-tuition services. These sometimes make use of the special regulations which allow dual registration of pupils. Parsons' 1999 report identifies a number of examples from around the country where effective reintegration work with permanently excluded children is possible.

The remainder (about 25,000 children) are receiving what has become known as 'education otherwise', which costs around four times as much as the average mainstream place. Schemes and programmes designed to meet the needs of children out of school are proliferating, with limited effective co-ordinating guidance on their management. This confuses attempts to quantify accurately and describe comprehensively the current situation. For instance, some children in Parsons' sample were probably counted more than once. Some authorities contract out the delivery of alternative provision, or make collaborative arrangements with other agencies. In some cases as an economy measure pupils on home-tuition programmes are being taught in groups, with little formal regulation.

Of PRUs, the Office for Standards in Education said: *'It is hardly possible to over-state the importance of the work that PRUs do …,'* but regrettably *'… few PRUs do so at all adequately, and few are appropriately supported in their efforts'* (OfSTED, 1993).

As Parsons points out, in many PRUs the pupils are a *mélange* of excluded and difficult children, non-attenders and truants, pregnant schoolgirls, those awaiting placement, and many others for whom a school place is not available. This heterogeneous group of pupils will lack commitment to the unit, and the planning of a coherent educational programme – both individually and as a whole – must be a nightmare. But, crucially, peer-bonding between pupils will happen almost overnight, and small groups of disaffected pupils may then collaborate in disruptive and delinquent activities which make it almost impossible to drive forward a remedial programme for the individual.

Home tuition, which is still the staple provision of some local education authorities hard pressed to meet their statutory obligations to out-of-school children in their area, provides barely five hours' tuition on average. Such services are scarcely audited or supervised, and it is doubtful whether much is achieved by them.

Based on a survey carried out by Mitchell (1966), reasons given for the exclusion of children were as follows:

- one child in three was excluded for disruption;

- one in four was excluded for physical abuse;

- one in five was excluded for verbal abuse;

- one in eight was excluded for not attending (is this a paradox?);

- one in 15 was excluded for criminal activities.

The Social Exclusion Unit (SEU, 1998) breaks the statistics down slightly differently:

- bullying and fighting – 30 per cent;

- disruption, misconduct and 'unacceptable behaviour' – 17 per cent;

- verbal abuse to peers – 15 per cent;

- verbal abuse to staff – 12 per cent;

- theft – 6 per cent;

- defiance and disobedience – 5 per cent;

- drugs – 4 per cent;

- physical abuse and assaults on staff – 1.2 per cent;

- other – 9.8 per cent.

The claim has been made that exclusions are necessary to protect staff, though it is clear from the SEU's figures that assaults on staff are a tiny proportion of the total.

One in three permanent exclusions were for disruptive behaviour. Try replacing the words 'disruptive behaviour' with the words 'trying to communicate needs, using non-verbal and verbal methods, which were found to be incomprehensible'. Now the problem is not 'How do we stop the child's behaviour?' but rather 'How do we translate what the child is trying to communicate into something understandable?'. This is an important change of emphasis; hopefully, as the reader digests this book, translation will become much easier.

Other groups in which there is a disproportionately high rate of exclusion are those with special needs, travellers, young carers, pregnant schoolgirls and teenage mothers. The DfEE *Social Inclusion: Pupil Support* guide (1999) also highlights the needs of 'those from families under stress', and pupils in transition from one Key Stage to another.

Imich (1994) found that a minority of schools exclude the majority of pupils. This cannot be passed off simply as a function of the pupil intake. It is more likely that some schools are better at managing problem pupils – perhaps because they are better at recruiting staff. Whilst schools as community resources are a collective responsibility, it cannot be acceptable that, as Parfrey (1977) says: *'Excluded children ... are at risk of becoming the scapegoats of a system that cannot cope'* (p. 117). A recent OfSTED report (1993) suggests that their inspectors held a similar view.

▓ DfEE guidance – *Social Inclusion: Pupil Support*

The DfEE recently issued new guidelines for dealing with exclusion, truancy and pupil support (DfEE, 1999).The main change is that the advice now has the force of law in that head teachers and governors must have regard to it when making decisions about exclusion. However, the core of that guidance, the grounds on which a pupil may be excluded, are virtually unchanged: exclusion should be used 'only in response to serious breaches of a school's policy on behaviour' (mention of the criminal law has been dropped from the new guidelines); it should be used as a last resort when all other reasonable steps have been taken (the new guidelines spell out in more detail the kinds of steps it envisages), and when allowing the child to remain in school would be seriously detrimental to the education or welfare of the pupil or others. Exclusion is not appropriate for minor misconduct, such as occasional failure to do homework or failure to bring dinner money. Pregnancy is not in itself sufficient reason for exclusion.

Custom and practice currently varies widely. From time to time anecdotal accounts circulate about exclusions for minor issues such as wearing non-regulation trainers, a pupil permanently excluded for threatening another pupil with a small empty plastic bottle, a 7-year-old excluded for sticking her tongue out at a teacher, or someone wearing a nose-stud, dreadlocks or having 'tramlines' shaved into hair. These exclusions at least should now be illegal.

Whilst the DfEE is clearly looking to go beyond the narrow concerns of hardline pedagogy, the emphasis is ambivalent, and the guidance is not particularly confident. Take paragraph 5.4: Let's involve parents (three cheers), by inviting them to a formal meeting with a representative of the LEA (no, make that two cheers). Consider paragraph 6.3: head teachers must consider all the facts carefully before giving an exclusion – but there is no mention of parental involvement *prior* to decision-making.

The guidance makes recourse to case studies of good practice. However, they are notably absent in many sections. A number of at-risk groups are identified, but no examples at all are given of projects for traveller's, 'young carers', children from families under stress, or even children from ethnic minorities. The case example for children in care describes the setting up of a committee to review their needs – this is hardly revolutionary. One helpful suggestion is to nominate a teacher to maintain liaison with carers and social services.

On a more positive note, the significance of transitions is now recognised and a checklist of factors associated with higher risk of failure after transition into the secondary phase is provided:

- a record of discipline problems;

- irregular attendance;

- emotional instability, poor social skills, low self-esteem;

- withdrawn behaviour;

- poor peer relationships;

- difficulty with the curriculum.

The guidance also highlights the importance of parental involvement, but does not say what their role is (other than to be 'informed' of various matters), why this is so important, or how they can be encouraged or persuaded to get involved. In fact, the guidance talks about parents mostly in the way old-style social services documents used to talk (and regrettably sometimes still do) about children in care – as if the parents are simply pawns who can be moved from one square to another at will, and on demand. There is no mention of sending single mums the bus fare if the meeting is the day before Giroday! In fact, no specific examples at all are given of good practice in home–school liaison. A few of the case studies show reductions in permanent exclusions, but not enough to inspire confidence.

Perhaps the DfEE was worried that it would go too far and seem unrealistic. To those who have been on the other side, the guidance may seem a little weak on actualities. However, despite these detailed criticisms, the report has strong points. It makes a good departure point, and constructs a comprehensive framework for concern. The emphasis is on early intervention and prevention through multi-agency working, partnership with parents (notwithstanding the previous criticisms) and a new concept – the Pastoral Support Programme (PSP).

The PSP is a school-based intervention which a named staff member will oversee. The guidance specifically states that the PSP does not replace the SEN assessment process (and see the discussion under 'code of practice' elsewhere). It is also encouraging to note that the DfEE wants 'administration to be kept to a minimum' (para. 5.1). A number of other agencies may be involved including social services and, importantly, the housing department, but curiously not including the Educational Welfare Service (EWS) or Educational Psychology Service (EPS). Perhaps this is an oversight, or perhaps these services are seen as part of the SEN framework rather than as pastoral support. A number of quite exciting exceptions are suggested, including disapplying the National Curriculum, joint registration in school and PRU or other unit, a managed move to another school for a fresh start, and support for specialist intervention such as bereavement or alcohol counselling. But the two examples given are a little unimaginative, reinforcing the idea that this is all rather new and untried.

So, in summary, the guidance provides a firm, fair and thorough framework attached to some advice on practical initiatives, and is rather tentative in tone.

League tables

Many people believe that the pressure to maintain and improve the school's league table position discourages many schools from taking a more inclusive and supportive approach. As the competition hots up, the temptation to exclude pupils who are likely to fail academically or appear to have a detrimental effect on the progress of others also increases. To discourage this, the DfEE recently announced that it intended to oblige schools to include the GCSE results of permanently excluded pupils in their returns. As for the league table, raw GCSE results are currently used which discount lower grades, and do not measure 'improvement'. One way to do this is to use so-called YELLIS (Year 11 Information System) scores which show how much children have progressed between entering the school and leaving. Schools awarded the DfEE 'progress measure' have achieved above average improvement between KS3 assessment and GCSE. However, neither of these measures fully reflect the efforts of schools who see themselves as a community resource with a pastoral role, encouraging the development of citizenship. It will also not reflect the numbers of immigrant children with English as an additional language, and children with other special needs.

The 'league-tables excuse' may, in any case, be more of a rationalisation which provides a good excuse for what the school wants to do anyway. It is almost impossible to assess, since the explanation is always used in the third person – i.e. 'other schools must be excluding children for that reason, but we would never dream of it!'

In future, exclusion statistics will be broken down by ethnic group. The DfEE intends to ask LEAs to collect data on fixed-term exclusions of five days or more, in order to set targets for reducing them. There is the obvious danger that schools will be able to reduce the five-day rate by giving out more four-day exclusions. The government also plans to collect data on the educational achievement of children being educated out of school. This is likely to show that educational achievements are poor, but it may be more difficult to know what they might have been under other circumstances.

■ Elective exclusion

On the other hand, behavioural problems may often be used by pupils as a way to lever themselves out of school obligations because they have fallen behind and are not being helped sufficiently to catch up. For these pupils, academic study seems irrelevant or overwhelming, often invoking the plaintive explanation that their lack of motivation is because 'school's boring'.

Here we can see the basis for a classic stand-off: the school tells the pupil 'you are a liability', and the pupil tells the school *'you don't help me enough, and anyway school's boring, in fact I hate it'*. This is a catch-all phrase which covers some of the following:

- I am going to fail and I can't face it.

- Don't you realize how tough adulthood is!

- I am scared. You tell me I will never succeed in life without all these GCSEs, and then you make it so hard I can't cope.

- I want to work but I am so confused.

In an ethnic context this sort of response can become a group-norm. Signithia Fordham (1987) observed black schoolchildren from low-income backgrounds in an American city. Her findings suggested that these children saw themselves as different and separate from others, and this reinforced the idea of 'brotherhood' and 'sisterhood' between children from the same ethnic background who otherwise would not have seen themselves as a group at all ('fictive kinship'). This had its positive aspects, but also encouraged the development of a barrier between the ethnic-minority children and the wider community. The children disapproved of any behaviour by one of their 'kin' which threatened the survival of the 'group'. This can be contrasted with the sense of 'healthy competition' between classmates from the majority ethnic group, and the tendency of these children to seek out those with whom they can more strongly identify, on the basis of family and socioeconomic background, ability and expectations for the future.

Fordham concluded that these black children had developed an 'oppositional social identity', setting themselves apart as different by adopting antisocial patterns of behaviour. Apart from giving the children a sense of being 'in with the group', it also reflected their feeling that they were second-class citizens, which arose from being poor and black in America. However, their oppositional behaviour had a negative impact on school achievement.

In contrast to this, consider the following study which shows how minority cultures can cope with saturation by a dominant larger culture without becoming overwhelmed. This is applicable to more recent migrant groups. The Tolai people of the Gazelle Peninsula (in North Eastern New Britain, part of Papua New Guinea) found themselves caught up in the process of colonial change, and had to absorb western culture into their own during the early part of this century. The Tolai were a large group who viewed their traditional way of life as superior to that in the West, but at the same time they wanted to be able to take hold of the material resources of the missionaries, government officials and business organisations coming into their community. Western officials quickly came to see the Tolai as a 'musical people', and the Tolai seized on this and created a cultural myth of musical superiority. 'Pipal Bilong Music Tru' is pidgin English for 'A Truly Musical People'.

This myth became something which they could build on as a community. It gave them a sense of self-worth, a sense of identity, and a direction in which to move. Through it, they developed new cultural styles which gave them access to a wider audience and paid off in terms of gaining equal access to knowledge and power of the outside world. The Tolai people have continued to take advantage of the political opportunities which have followed on from this, and through determination and struggle have seen the myth become a reality. This has given their culture a cohesiveness and sense of identity which has enabled them to absorb western influences without losing themselves in the process.

Actually the African–Caribbean community has had quite a head start on many of the more recent arrivals; and although the situation is still far from ideal, they are at least beginning to access real power and influence. The government recently appointed its first black female peer to the cabinet. Ebuchi's fascinating examination of Polish migration into North America during the latter part of the nineteenth century suggests that many decades and perhaps as much as a century is needed for migrant subcultures to establish themselves in a host culture.

This may seem far removed from the concerns of a school

management team, but for once the cliché that 'school is the world in miniature' is meaningful here. The key messages here are:

- Pupils will seek a peer group identity for themselves and may define it antisocially if they see no alternatives.

- Groups who can establish a sustaining mythology which identifies them positively will advance more quickly and establish a better raport with the host culture.

- Political power (in pupil terms, 'having a voice', representation on school councils, involvement in parent–teacher associations and school events, governorship and so on) is hard-won by minorities. However, power-sharing coalesces splinter groups and reduces internal conflict.

Teachers and communication

Children come to be seen as 'failing' when pupil–staff relationships deteriorate. As with any other failing relationship, communication has broken down and both sides are resorting to the megaphone. Teachers want to help but for many reasons they are struggling to do so. The main problem is that it is difficult to 'translate' behaviour, which is a form of communication, accurately enough to formulate an appropriate response. Teachers say:

- they need more external support for learning and behavioural needs;

- there are too few specialist staff;

- there is insufficient time and skills to deal with behavioural difficulties in the mainstream;

- they need far more training in handling behavioural problems;

- they are unsure how to tell the difference between naughtiness, behaviour which is communication, and behaviour arising from deep-seated emotional disturbance or abuse.

Evaluating interventions

The value of outreach work with families and children can extend beyond immediate outcomes by its influence on conduct of parents and home lifestyle. Sceptics might well dismiss this, but a common sense view must be that we all need support and advice, encouragement and sympathy, material assistance, moral support and companionship, and someone to help from time to time with the 'hands-on' demands of parenting. This supplements our own skills knowledge, ability and resources, particularly during times of crisis. Most of us have a small network of people who provide this. How well would we manage without? For those who do not – is there understanding and real concern, or rejection and condemnation?

The cost of social failure is high. Farrington's (1996) influential work on the development of offending and antisocial behaviour makes it clear that specific factors in childhood do predict future problems. One of the factors he identifies is low attainment in school, and this obviously correlates highly with poor attendance and exclusion. Farrington also stresses that the learning problems start in infancy, and better assessment, identification and remedial action is strongly indicated.

Excluded education provision is expensive, and there may be additional health and social care costs resulting from poor self-care and self-help skills. The ultimate point of social failure is reached when incarceration becomes necessary. The cost of prison care is extraordinarily high. Intervention programmes (which address needs earlier in the life cycle, when problems are still school-based), will be more cost-effective than prison, even those with a low success rate. The real problem lies in shifting resources from the treatment side (post-18) to the prevention side (pre-18). Who should fund intervention programmes? In an ideal world, it would be funded by the agencies which benefit. This may be the health service, HM Prisons, or one of many other social agencies. But at the moment the paymaster appears to be education, and any school-based programme for excluded children must enable them to meet their statutory obligations as cost effectively as possible.

The current government appears to have taken this message on board, and resources are beginning to be targeted on reducing reported rates on two key indicators – one is truancy and the other is exclusion.

One influential MP was quoted as saying: *'There are no votes in prevention, but there are in punishment.'* It is certainly the case that early interventions (in this context, anything happening within statutory school age, but often taken to mean during the primary phase), implemented as a preventative measure, are more speculative than punishment after the fact.

Issues which need to be explored are:

■ Is there a relationship between school exclusion and serious crime?

■ Is there a relationship between school exclusion and minor offending?

■ Will intervention to reduce school exclusions also reduce either minor offending or serious crime?

■ What are the financial implications?

■ Are there longer term financial benefits arising from early intervention programmes?

■ How can those benefits be calculated?

■ If there are benefits in early intervention services, how can the resources for these be fairly and effectively taken from the services which are benefiting and transferred to the service which provides them?

To take simplistic figures: the cost of prison incarceration at current levels is around £2000 per week per person. So reducing the prison population by one person for one year saves about £100,000. An early-intervention programme which can redirect a pupil away from permanent exclusion costs around £4000 per pupil (based on a recent evaluation of a Central London project). So an early-intervention programme which had even a comparatively low success rate could still save the public purse. But a programme which enabled a pupil to stay in school would not necessarily also keep that pupil out of prison in later life. The only way to get proof of effectiveness would be to carry out a longitudinal study. This would not take as long as one might think since, according to Farrington, most offending is carried out by people under 25 years of age:

'On average, official criminal careers began at age 17, lasted six years, ended at age 23, and included 4.5 offences leading to conviction. The men first convicted at the earliest ages tended to become the most persistent offenders, in committing large numbers of offences at high rates over long time periods.'
(Farrington, 1996)

In other words:

■ Fairly accurate predictions about longer term outcomes could be obtained by observing young people (particularly males) during the seven years following minimum school leaving age.

■ Persistent offenders take up much more police and court time, and lifelong offenders may spend many years in prison.

Still, the equations are complex, and likely to be controversial. Common sense suggests that the accumulated benefits of reduced offending, reduced unemployment, and reduced need for health and social services are also targets worth aspiring to.

The best evidence for the effectiveness of intervention is to see a young man who never gave the least indication that he had absorbed anything you tried to do for him when he was at school come back and show himself to you, with pride. The communication is still non-verbal, but appropriate, and the message is that the bond you had tried to forge and the commitment you had shown some years before had been an important catalyst in creating an adult who felt himself to be included in society.

So the benefits of a programme which tackles school failure and its underlying causes may be felt (both immediately and later on) within a wide social context, in areas which are the responsibility of other agencies such as the police, social workers and primary healthcare workers. How can a commissioning service (generally, education) be recompensed for the cost savings to those services which may result? At present, a good answer to what is a very good question does not appear to exist. It will become answerable, however, when the many interested parties come together to try to answer it. For the time being, whoever pays for the reintegration work needs to be able to compare directly costs of different strategies for the group of pupils who have special emotional and behavioural needs – those who are described elsewhere in this book as having social–relational disabilities. Figure 1 presents some relevant data.

Many services to children and families are mandated by moral, ethical and statutory obligations which require the delivery of provision deemed necessary, regardless of cost. Additionally, there are expectations as to quality. For instance, in deciding how to respond to emergencies, the cost of providing an ambulance service is not compared with the much cheaper cost of travel to hospital by bus, because service standards require a rapid response. Service standards in education require that a satisfactory educational provision is still made to permanently excluded children. Whether this is achieved in the majority of cases is doubtful

For one student:		
A reintegration project costs about –	£4000	
A PRU place per year costs on average	£7000	(DfEE estimate)
An EBD school place per year costs at least	£10,000	(local authority lists of charges)
Home tuition of 5 hours per week for a year costs	£6500	(based on £30/hour + on-costs)
Mean cost of 'continuing cases' of permanent exclusion in three test LEAs	£5134	(Parsons, 1996)
Mean indicative costs for full-year of equivalent education in six LEAs	£4336	(Parsons, 1996)

Figure 1

(Parsons, 1999). The successful reintegration of fixed-term exclusions back into the heart of their own school, or of permanently excluded pupils into mainstream schools, is a much better option than any of the typical alternatives. The reality is that provision is resources led and not needs led. Principles and pragmatism are at odds here.

The cost of a PRU place varies from authority to authority – as does the proportion of pupils diverted into each type of provision shown in Figure 1, the time spent out of school on differing provisions (varying from a few weeks to indefinitely), the likelihood that an excluded pupil will end up in provision for emotional and behavioural difficulties (EBD), the cost of special education, and so on.

▉ Are behavioural difficulties a form of disability?

A number of models of disability are currently in use. One useful distinction frequently made is between 'medical' and 'social' models of disability. Under the medical model, disability is seen as a result of the individual's condition. Society has an obligation to do something to alleviate the disability, but no responsibility for creating it. Under the social model, disability is seen as the result of an interaction between individual and society.

In some sense we are all 'disabled' in a varied range of situations. For instance, when domestic appliances break down or we need legal advice most of us turn to a 'support worker', such as an electrician or solicitor. We need assistance, but we do not call this 'disability' because the majority of us suffer from the condition. On the other hand, doorways are an important factor for those in wheelchairs, and when they are very heavy can act as a deterrent to entry. An anecdotal report that commissionaires in a major British university complained recently about 'having to open the doors' for a wheelchair-bound pupil confirms that, even at a basic level, attitudes are very much at variance with the idea of an inclusive society.

So disability is a function of both individual and institutional circumstances, as Figure 2 attempts to demonstrate. The medical model is still useful, however, because disability is not only socially constructed, but also sometimes more realistically viewed as a function of 'given' or immutable conditions.

▉ Exclusion is a socially constructed problem

Whilst some of the obstacles to inclusion derive from individual limitations, there is a moral obligation for the education system to

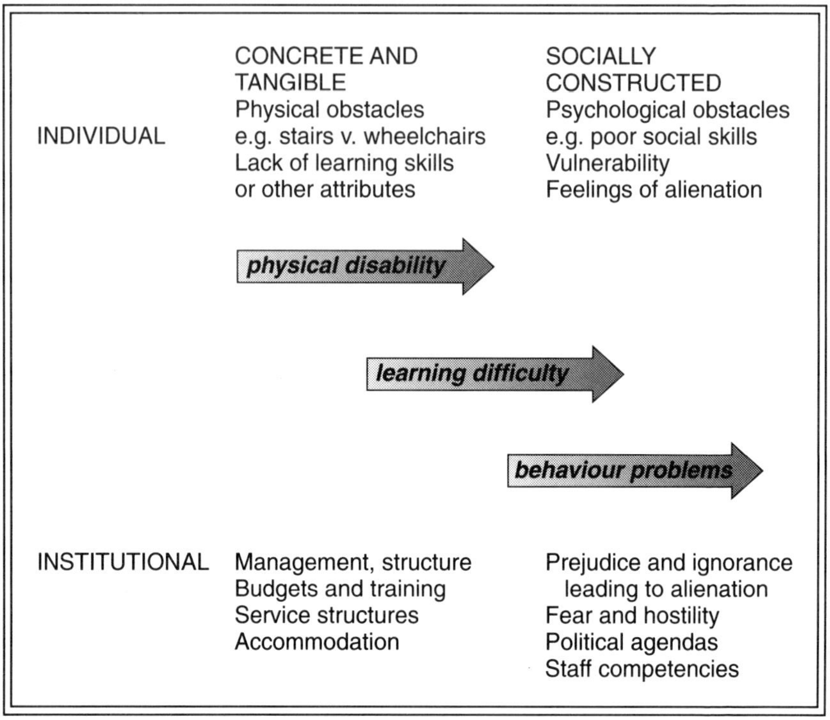
CONCRETE AND TANGIBLE
SOCIALLY CONSTRUCTED
INDIVIDUAL
Physical obstacles
e.g. stairs v. wheelchairs
Lack of learning skills
or other attributes
Psychological obstacles
e.g. poor social skills
Vulnerability
Feelings of alienation
physical disability
learning difficulty
behaviour problems
INSTITUTIONAL
Management, structure
Budgets and training
Service structures
Accommodation
Prejudice and ignorance
leading to alienation
Fear and hostility
Political agendas
Staff competencies

Figure 2

address these as well as institutional impediments. Furthermore, all the 'constructed' items listed in Figure 2 are psychological and frequently reflect attitudes which are based on ignorance. Some particular conditions of behavioural difficulty would fall in the 'tangible and individual' sector of this diagram and may well remain intractable for a very long time to come. Some individuals might prefer to remain segregated, and the ethical paradox of enforced inclusion may well become an issue.

However, for the vast majority of pupils excluded for behavioural problems, their needs fall squarely into the right-hand side and the lower half of the diagram. *Exclusion is a constructed and mainly institutional problem.*

There are many obstacles placed in the way of a child at risk of permanent exclusion who wants to 'reintegrate' into his or her school (marginalised children feel a sense of social exclusion long before they are physically rejected). The child's history, the causes of failure which have not been successfully addressed, and the powerful sense of failure and rejection carried by both child and family are three such obstacles.

Although there may be grounds for claiming that the exclusion was merited, there is still a moral obligation for the education system to intervene more humanely. The child's problems are frequently the result of unhelpful attitudes, ignorance and stressful domestic circumstances, and these may be amenable to change, given the right change agent. Some particular behavioural difficulties may be more intractable, and realistic objectives must be set by schools. For the vast majority of pupils excluded for behavioural problems, the causal factors run like genetic threads through individuals, families and institutions. As a community we should start by recognising our mutual responsibility.

How can social exclusion and 'disability' be related?

■ The term 'disability' is appropriate here because the terminology to which it gives rise – and in particular the medical/social distinction outlined above – fits the situation very well. Excluded pupils are generally, and wrongly, considered to be the sole architects of their own misfortune.

■ The 'default' terminology (which I suppose is couched in terms of juvenile delinquency) has simply formed around public or professional opinion based on no particular evidence.

■ Those who want to change the consensus are entitled to adopt an alternative terminology if it can be backed up by direct evidence and first-hand experience.

■ Such an approach effectively places the issue of behavioural difficulties clearly within a logical framework which allows the development of a coherent and ideologically well-founded approach to the problem of behaviourally challenging pupils.

Schools are becoming increasingly accessible to, and accessed by, pupils with physical and learning disabilities. However, for some, the discontinuity between their individual needs and the social and physical environment is still too great for their inclusion to be viable. The dividing line between these two groups can and will shift towards greater inclusion, as skills and resources develop and attitudes and awareness change. *Exactly the same kind of analysis can and should be applied to those with behavioural difficulties.*

It should be acknowledged that there is a fragmented third group of the mildly disabled, who could be included in a mainstream school setting, but for various reasons are denied this option. The evidence would suggest that too many pupils with behavioural difficulties find themselves in this third group.

One possible justification for framing exclusion as disability rather than framing 'delinquency' might lie in the psychological concept of 'multiple intelligence'. Howard Gardner (1983, 1995) challenged the assumption that intelligence could be measured as a single psychological dynamic, and suggested there might be seven different aspects of intelligence – linguistic, logical–mathematical, spatial, musical, bodily kinaesthetic, interpersonal (ability to relate to, and understand, others) and intrapersonal (self-awareness, and the ability to develop effective ideas of identity and personhood).

One major issue is how to set about measuring these qualities in a systematic way. In the absence of such measures we could only guess that a pupil lacked interpersonal or intrapersonal ability by outcome – in other words by his or her behaviour. Nevertheless, such a construct makes it possible to see how two pupils of similar background could respond very differently to similar circumstances, and underlines the need to have a clear idea of exactly who we have in mind, and what we mean, when we use the term 'excluded pupil'.

It is possible that some syndromes which are currently recognised as disorders – such as attention-deficit disorder, oppositional–defiant disorder, other emotional and conduct disorders, and social-anxiety disorder – should be re-examined from a social–relational viewpoint, and in terms of the child's perceptions of self and of 'others'.

Such an approach recognises that issues of power and control figure greatly in the circumstances of the 'socially disabled', and that behaviour towards adults is surprisingly contingent on the social cues which the adult gives, or fails to give. *When the right skills and approach are employed, it is surprisingly easy to turn a taciturn, aggressive or suspicious teenager into a dependent and vulnerable child, simply by providing the right social context.* This is relevant not only to pupil–staff relationships in school, but also to professional–pupil relationships in the context of intervention either before or after permanent exclusion.

Figure 3 may help to explain why this is a social–relational model of disability, so that a 'deficit' is not apparent all the time. The pupil will appear to be quite normal and co-operative except when particular 'trigger' events occur which are 'disabling', drastically reducing self-confidence and undermining coping skills. Examples of triggers might be: criticism of written work, threat of a delayed return home, implied criticism of family, or a situation involving perceived loss of self-esteem in front of peers. The resulting stress level may be mediated by other factors such as hunger, tiredness or hormonal fluctuations.

		The pupil has been placed under stress as part of a 'normal' school day	
		Yes?	No?
Social-relational disability has been triggered by one or more unknown events at home or at school	YES	SRD apparent	SRD *not* apparent
	NO	SRD *not* apparent	SRD *not* apparent

Figure 3

Triggers are likely to be themselves conditioned rather than innate, and so could take a very wide variety of forms. The pupil, under seemingly innocuous conditions, becomes difficult or argumentative, and removes co-operation. Teachers may become confused and defensive because they sense a 'trigger' has been activated, but they genuinely do not know what it is. The 'disability' remains hidden, because two or even three factors are required to activate it – the disability condition itself, the trigger, and other possible mediating factors such as tiredness or a recent argument at home.

In particular this last condition means that the same situation on another occasion passes unremarked, increasing the sense of unpredictability. Some teachers are much better than others at intuitively avoiding these triggers.

▪ Evidence for the existence of 'social–relational disability'

The term 'social–relational disability' has been coined to describe the dysfunctional condition of an individual who is ineffective or unskilled in relating either to others in different social contexts, or to himself or herself ('inner awareness'). Poor social–relational ability becomes apparent only in particular settings, under more or less limited circumstances. Currently, the evidence that some people may have a social–relational disability can be inferred from various facts:

- ▪ Some individuals conflict with others to their own detriment sufficiently frequently or seriously as to significantly impair their quality of life, under circumstances in which others from a similar background would not.

■ Pupils who are permanently excluded often deeply regret what has happened and show little understanding of their role in the events leading up to exclusion.

■ They often lack the emotional resilience required to cope with the pressure of everyday school life. This resilience is mediated by relationships with others, and also by the ability to reflect and learn from negative experiences.

■ Their parents frequently seem to show corresponding difficulties, and often have histories of social exclusion themselves.

■ Social circumstances and psychological assessment may give cause for concern, but do not show circumstances sufficiently serious to warrant referral to other agencies.

■ Both pupil and parent frequently have difficulty communicating – a core element in interpersonal relations.

People with social–relational disability have unusual difficulties in relating to others, in specific situations, which often involve higher levels of stress. They may also find inner awareness hard to achieve.

The involvement of families

Difficulties leading to exclusion arise from complex combinations of personal and family problems which cross the continuum of psychological, social and biological needs. They are incompatible with the relatively rigid institutions of the education system. Whilst education authorities and schools accept their responsibilities to the wider community, there are often ambivalent feelings about 'disruptive' or 'difficult' children, who pose problems which frequently seem to confound even the specialists. These children are not seen as 'disabled' but as a source of stress in teachers and fear in other children: causes, problems and solutions are all contentious.

When people lack specific skills, they often turn to their immediate family for support and guidance. Social skills are largely learned rather than innate, and it is likely that serious limitations in interpersonal or intrapersonal ability arise only when parents are unable to teach their children by example.

▆ The peer group

Interpersonal relationships for children revolve around the peer group (especially status) and social skills. These link to the child's inner awareness of identity, self-esteem, power/control, and sexuality. Stress levels will be higher for children who have (or think they have) shortcomings in these areas. This is especially true during adolescence. Additional pressures at home or school can trigger behaviours which appear to others to be disruptive and antisocial.

▆ Exclusion and 'special educational needs'

The *Special Educational Needs Code of Practice* (SENCoP) published in 1994 identifies five stages of assessment, planning and review which are designed to provide a phased and controlled approach to the management and alleviation of 'special' educational problems. The categorisation of individuals into stereotypical 'problem categories' is rejected in favour of uniquely designed solutions which are specific to the individual, and reflect a continuity of need.

The five stages are characterized by: (1) class-teacher intervention; (2) senior-manager intervention; (3) outside-agency intervention; (4) request for a comprehensive statutory assessment; and (5) the completion of a formal statement of special educational needs.

A confusion has crept into current usage which awaits clarification – does the code apply to pupils with behavioural difficulties? An excluded child automatically comes to the attention of educational agencies outside a mainstream school environment, in order to access the continuing educational provision to which the law entitles him or her. In terms of stages, this would imply that the pupil is at least at stage 3, although that is probably not quite what the writers of the *Code of Practice* were envisaging. However, the terminology of special needs is often not applied to excluded children, whose difficulties may be viewed as falling outside the framework provided by the *Code*. Nevertheless, the *Code*'s rigorous expectations should apply to both groups, because the philosophy which underpins it can be very appropriately applied to the excluded pupil.

Let us be clear here. Many authorities would claim – with some justification – that they do include behavioural difficulties within their code of practice, and where an outside agency is called in this is seen as 'stage 3'. However, good practice in some boroughs is not mirrored everywhere. Secondly, learning difficulties have to be addressed within the *Code*, but a head teacher may pre-emptively exclude a pupil without reference to it. A code which is applied expediently only when it suits is no code at all. We are a long way from being able to manage behavioural difficulties proactively, and in a crisis the system breaks down (i.e. the pupil is excluded generally without real support or help for the problems which caused it). Finally, the lip service may be to the *Code* but the mindset is still retributive.

The *Code of Practice* is set to change around the end of 1999, apparently becoming simpler and less bureacratic. These changes are now overdue.

Reintegration

The primary objective of 'reintegration' is the management of personal development, encouraging a change in the behaviour of the excluded pupil by altering key elements in his or her lifestyle, outlook and skills. The overall goal is to expedite the achievement of the pupil's own educational goals by removing the impediments which prevent this. Reintegration work uniquely incorporates skills, knowledge and understanding from across the spectrum of professional services to clients; principally derived from education, but also social services, counselling and therapy, welfare, health, advice and advocacy, mentoring, coaching, psychology and service management.

Reintegration exists as a process in its own right. The boundaries of activity, based in good professional practice, go beyond the accountabilities of any one profession. Reintegration requires multi-skilled workers.

The objective of any intervention is limited to achieving educational goals, and interventions are structured to achieve these limited objectives. Pupils on a reintegration programme are not being 'trained how to behave'; they are discovering how to achieve their own objectives through understanding (especially the understanding of their own behaviour), and their parents are receiving guidance in how to help them do this (partly but not exclusively how to manage their child's behaviour more effectively).

3 Excluded children and excluded families

Inexplicable motivation explained

What is it that motivates a pupil to pursue a course – in the face of warnings, intermediate sanctions, advice and intervention – leading to permanent eviction from his or her main non-domestic environment? The fact that it happens at all is a commentary on the depersonalising condition of society. Their behaviour is a symptom, and not the disease itself. Expectations of pupil behaviour are extraordinarily high – to arrive punctually and sit silently through hour after hour of study (but to participate when required), to accept discipline without complaint even where it seems unjust, unnecessary or excessively demeaning, not to exercise the right of freedom of movement around the environment and not to exercise the right to have a bad day without anyone commenting or criticising.

Adults allow themselves a degree of flexibility which accommodates their idiosyncratic needs. This is very seldom accorded to children. During days of high stress or anxiety or simply out of boredom, adults walk about, vent their feelings, take a break, have a snack, switch tasks, talk things over with colleagues, and so on. Job changes relieve the tedium and help to ensure that individuals can gravitate towards employment and a social environment which matches their personality. The freedom to do so is a key factor in employment satisfaction.

In this light it is not surprising that a marginalized proportion of the school population is unable to cope. Behavioural problems at school are a response to circumstances which are creating dysphoric states – high anxiety, depression, anger, despair, fear, confusion, and so on. These states are exacerbated by the need to adopt a rigid and highly disciplined routine at school.

John (1996) identified five important pupil–staff factors which were cited by pupils as relevant to their exclusion:

- lack of respect;

- unfair decisions;

- being humiliated;

- experiencing racism (and/or gender bias);

- unjustified physical contact.

The pupils' self-perceptions of the causes of their own behaviour were grouped by her under five headings as:

- having a laugh;

- maintaining a 'reputation';

- pupils' lack of aptitude for schooling;

- a response to sanctions imposed;

- a way of raising profile ('notice of self').

How does this fit into a social–relational disability framework? Firstly, the social–relational model is only a 'model' and is not designed to explain every exclusion. Each of the first five factors identified by John can be seen as actually present or only perceived as present. No-one could dispute, for instance, that some teachers, however small that number might be, hold racist views. At the same time, it is all too easy for a pupil to interpret a teacher's sanctions as inspired by their race rather than their behaviour. Where there is racism, or any of the other pupil–staff factors, this is clearly wrong. However, the reactions of children with social–relational disability will be unwise and inept, and likely to lead to their own disadvantage. Children without social–relational disability will either not react or, occasionally, find a way to redress the balance effectively. The effect is also cumulative, so that a succession of small incidents involving the socially unskilled pupil, and teachers who are less accommodating and empathic, sets in train a cycle of inappropriate reaction, sanction, and the development of a label – 'problem child' (see Figure 4).

The self-perceptions of the excluded pupils are interesting. They might be interpreted as follows:

- *Having a laugh.* This behaviour is an attempt to establish a common identity, but is done in an unconstructive way.

- *Maintaining a 'reputation'.* Self-esteem is based mainly on receiving approval from others, but there is never quite enough perceived approval, necessitating further attention-seeking acts.

People who have a social–relational disability persistently use *social strategies* that are:

- ■ naive
- ■ ineffective
- ■ offensive.

The *consequences* include:

- ■ rejection by others
- ■ the imposition of sanctions
- ■ failure to achieve goals.

Figure 4

■ *Pupils' lack of aptitude for schooling.* Some pupils do badly at school, and don't mind at all! Probably, the social aspects of school life compensate. Where relationships are hard work and self-esteem is based on the perceived views of others, 'poor' academic results are evidence of inadequacy, creating a highly unpleasant social environment which the pupils may seek to avoid by self-excluding.

■ *A response to sanctions imposed.* Accepting criticism is quite a refined social skill, with which SRD pupils have difficulty.

■ *A way of raising profile ('notice of self').* Children seek attention for many different reasons. 'Nice' children do it by asking in the right way, waiting patiently, and learning to approach the teacher at times when he or she is accessible. Again, these are sophisticated social skills. Children who cannot work out how to attract attention positively do so negatively. Anyway, how many times can a pupil say to a teacher: 'Please help me, I can't do it', before both teacher and pupil give up in frustration?

This is the kind of thing Parfrey (1997) was commenting on when he suggested that children were being scapegoated because the *system* could not cope. Many children need more help to keep up than they are currently getting, and too many resources are tied up in expensive special education.

Figure 5 shows three categories of causation, not three categories of child. A particular child might show elements of two or three categories, or indeed fit tightly into a single category.

A pupil whose presenting problems are *school phobic* has a dislike or fear of school and has realised that, whilst truants are coerced to return

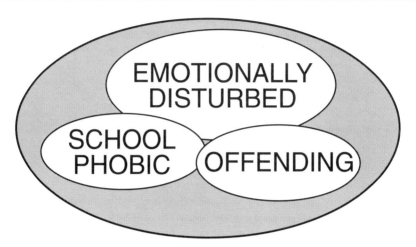

Figure 5

to school, excludees are given strict instructions to stay away. Starting with misbehaviour which merits time out of class, the pupil learns how to get time out of school, and eventually the process reaches its logical conclusion. Parents often collude (sometimes unconsciously) with pupils who do not attend. Self-excludees may not acknowledge or even be aware that they have chosen this route to avoid school, until challenged. The case studies of Aleem and Shane in Appendix 1 are examples of this.

Pupils are sometimes formally diagnosed as 'school phobic'. Diagnostic criteria vary, and the term in this context is used simply to describe someone in whom a dislike or fear of school has become generalised, rather than a 'psychiatric disorder'. Where fears are directly related to specific events or people, and pupils have enough self-awareness to recognise this and tell someone, appropriate action can be taken. School-phobic behaviour arises in children who:

- have avoidant personalities and who find it hard to confront negative aspects in themselves;

- cannot 'reflect inwardly' or find the process too painful;

- have fears or dislikes that are now displaced (or disconnected) from the earlier experiences on which they were based.

A pupil whose presenting problem is *emotional disturbance* often finds it difficult to maintain the boundary between school and personal life. Home and family may not be providing nurture and support (see John's case study in Appendix 1), or some aspects of school life are triggering a powerful emotional reaction (see Nathan, Appendix 1). For either reason, the pupil's view of self is tarnished from within, and the stresses of daily life drain emotional resources, leaving him or her unable to cope with additional stress in school. As the strain begins to show, much effort is dissipated trying to maintain an image, and gain peer approval. A series of involuntary outbursts or unwise confrontations further undermines confidence on all sides and the pupil is in due course excluded. Sometimes disturbed pupils use conflict as an excuse to leave the site either with or without a formal exclusion as a means of escape, although after a rest they can be very keen to return to school.

A pupil whose presenting problems are delinquent has become involved with a peer group, usually outside school and frequently consisting of older children, whose behaviour is antisocial and anti-authoritarian. School life becomes more difficult as the demands of the peer group and lack of parental control interfere with healthy habits such as getting to bed at a reasonable time (see Hamed, Appendix 1). Peer approval is often won by offending, and the pupil may come to the attention of the police. Drug and substance abuse further disrupts an academic perspective. As school time is lost through oversleeping or non-attendance, and attention starts to wander when in school, school life becomes increasingly marginalised in the life of the pupil (and vice versa). The authority of the school is weakened as the counter-culture of street life assumes a predominant position in the pupil's outlook. Sooner or later a conflict will occur between a teacher who requires 'respect' and the pupil who no longer feels required to show it. Delinquent pupils generally electively non-attend or deliberately set up their permanent exclusion.

It is not the behaviour itself which identifies the category, but the meaning behind it. For instance, pupils may self-exclude because they are either delinquent, phobic or disturbed, but the rationale in each case – and hence the response – needs to be different. This is why behavioural interventions do not always work. The presenting problems of pupils seldom fit only one category; for instance a phobic pupil may also be disturbed, have great difficulty coping whilst in school, and be unaware of manipulating the system to reduce the stress level.

Learning deficits

Children fail at school for a variety of reasons and failure to learn does not necessarily result in behaviour problems. Skaalvik (1993) found that lack of confidence in slow-learners could lead to a range of self-injurious behaviours in the class which he identified as self-protective mechanisms, such as:

■ non-involvement;

■ disruptive manipulation;

■ preoccupation with self;

■ lack of effort.

These activities increased in settings involving a high degree of social comparison (such as participatory activities).

The extent and severity of under-achievement on school-based activities will be reflected in the degree to which pupils say 'school is sh!t'. This apparent aversion to school will also be affected by involvements with non-school activities such as street culture or employment, as well as by school phobic factors. Although any perceived inadequacies, such as poor football skills, could create an aversion to attending school, the chronic stress posed to intellectually able pupils by the threat of exposure of perceived inadequacy is likely to prove more important.

A pupil who has a problem about feeling inadequate will see the prospect of low grades in GCSEs as sufficient reason to look for a way out. *There is only one way open to children who want to opt out of school – permanent exclusion.*

Reduced work-rate through off-task behaviour and preoccupation with problems, and reduced attention arising from anxious distraction, will also inhibit progress. Low expectation may lead to low motivation. Parental aspiration is an important factor in both, and parents who failed in school may have no aspirations for their own children. The completion of homework, another indicator of successful schooling, may be undermined by a chaotic or disturbed home environment.

Pupils who feel bad find it harder to stay on task, but their cognitive abilities when on task are also impaired.

Ability to retrieve information may be affected by mood, and there are several examples of studies showing that positive feelings increase creativity and problem-solving ability (e.g. Isen, 1993). Teachers need to know this, even if it is hard to incorporate this knowledge into their practice.

Reduced attendance by virtue of illness, absenteeism, internal exclusions (such as the 'withdrawal room'), external exclusion, and permanent exclusion will impede progress and delay learning. One report suggested that a primary-age child waits an average of 14 weeks to receive an average of three hours weekly of home tuition (Joseph Rowntree Foundation, 1994). The educational impact of even quite short exclusions can have a disastrous effect on progress, especially for pupils bumping along the lower margin of achievement. For instance, missing key lessons in which new methods, or core elements, in a new programme of study are covered can result in confusion and despair.

There is some evidence that absence from school can reduce intelligence quota (IQ) scores, and presumably therefore supposedly innate ability (Ceci, 1991). Ceci also cites a number of studies from different cultures and decades suggesting that irregular schooling, delayed onset and early termination of schooling is detrimental to IQ, and that variation in aptitude as measured by IQ and in achievement are broadly equally correlated with amount of schooling. IQ and achievement, therefore, can both be affected by a range of environmental and social factors. The excluded pupil may have become trapped long before exclusion in a downward spiral of circumstantial impediments to learning, and consequential failure.

Vygotsky and the zone of proximal development

Vygotsky, a Russian educationalist, coined the term 'zone of proximal development' at the beginning of the twentieth century. It is a concept that has outlived its inventor and it is one of those ideas which many people have heard of but few can define. The zone of proximal development is simply the gap between what a learner can achieve independently and what can be achieved with help from the teacher. It is relevant to this discussion because it reinforces the view that learning is usually a socially contextualised event, which cannot be fully described in purely individual terms. Disruptive pupils can exist only in a context which accommodates them, and pupils who cannot learn are more likely to be off-task.

Trauma, rejection and vulnerability

In dealing with excluded children there is an additional problem– the sense of loss and rejection which many pupils feel as a result. This may reflect their need to be victims and to express a wider sense of loss and rejection. The role of loss of all kinds (including the way emergent identities in children can collapse during the processes of socialisation) is little understood, partly because reactions to specific situations varies so much from child to child. Socially–relationally disabled children are unlucky in that their personalities make it difficult for them to cope with some combinations of school processes and life events. From this view, excluded children are truly a special group, suffering from an unrecognised condition.

A comparison may be made with the view taken of autistic children before the syndrome was described and recorded by Kanner in 1943. Was their behaviour viewed as insane, delinquent, or at any rate deliberate? Of course, there are no descriptions of autistic children prior to this date, because the condition was not recognised, and so we can never know. Where Tourette's syndrome has been diagnosed a statement is likely to be considered appropriate; but, just as Asperger's syndrome is a mild form of autism, is it possible that some children have a mild form of Tourette's syndrome? These suggestions may be completely speculative. However, what can be stated with more confidence is that there is a continuing progression in our understanding of psychiatric conditions. In contrast, physical illnesses are usually caused by a specific organism, established treatments are uncontroversial, new treatments can be evaluated systematically, and prognosis is generally consistent. There is far less agreement as to the provenance and taxonomy of mental health problems

Mental ill-health is amorphously defined, generally by the presence of clusters of symptoms or behaviour. The presence or absence of a particular item is often a matter of clinical judgment, and the way the 'rules' are interpreted to arrive at a diagnosis is subject to individual variation, and may be contentious. For instance in one case, a consultant diagnosed attention-deficit disorder, even though problems had not emerged prior to the age of seven, as specified in the manual.

The diagnosis of recognised syndromes and disorders is uncertain; and the possible existence of unrecognised conditions resulting in problem behaviour at school cannot be ruled out. *Whilst this may not help much in deciding what to do about the problem, it should be borne in mind by decision-makers when they are deciding the future schooling of a boy who should be seen, first, as an innocent victim of himself.*

Pupils who have substantial and clearly defined clinical profiles will be picked up by the educational psychology services, and their transfer to alternative establishments will follow, routed via the statementing procedure.

The much greyer areas between health and instability are better understood from a functional point of view. That is, given a particular set of behaviours, what is the best way of managing the pupil who is displaying them?

Skilled and competent teachers are willing and able to learn how to adapt to their pupils' needs, taught by the pupils themselves – it is an interactive process. Understanding the meaning of behaviour is one of the main tasks. Generally, excluded children are not mentally ill, unless you count adolescence as an illness.

▓▓ Pupils in transition to Key Stage 4

Key Stage 4 (KS4) starts at the beginning of Year 10 and lasts for two years, culminating in GCSE exams. The whole of the key stage is assessed in this way, and on-going formal assessments are made throughout the two years, some of which form part of the continuous-assessment element in final results. The academic pressure is much greater than at any other key stage. Teacher expectations are elevated, workload (especially homework) increases, and there is a greater emphasis on self-study skills. A different ethos often prevails in KS4. How this is formalised will depend on the terminology used and the structure of the school. For instance, there may or may not be an A level department. In some schools, 'upper school' refers only to A level groups, whereas in others it also includes KS4. Choices for optional subjects are generally finalised in the Easter term of Year 9. In the summer term of Year 9, KS3 Standard Assessment Tasks (SATs) are taken in May and pupils may be encouraged to view these tests as part of the preparations for the GCSE courses to come.

Pupils will thus start to receive information relevant to this transition in the two terms leading up to the summer term of KS3. Some of this information provides cues that are likely to raise motivation, but for some this raises anxiety. These cues may be acting as 'triggers', provoking the kinds of reaction which lead to permanent exclusion. The pupil's behaviour is showing that, for whatever reason, the challenge of KS4 is creating sufficient anxiety and attempts may be made to avoid or reject it.

We frequently underestimate the stress involved in transitional processes. We know that changing jobs is very high on the list of adult stressors. Why should it be any different for adolescents? Recent research has also shown that, at times of transition, unresolved emotional issues (often related to bereavement and loss) can surface, leaving pupils struggling with a turbulent period of anxiety, depression, restlessness, identity crisis, loss of confidence, or 'searching' behaviour.

For some, prospects of a change are too overwhelmingly terrifying – these are the ones who are permanently excluded at the end of Year 9. For others, the stress builds up over the first term or two of Year 10. Others, of course, manage to adapt to KS4 ('not as scary as they thought it would be') and settle down. There are really two options here:

- ■ *Option 1.* Recognise the internal struggle in which the pupil is engaged, and accommodate the child with support and empathy. Provide mentors, set up self-help groups, reduce anxiety by structuring the transition, and help each pupil (in partnership with the family) to come to terms with his or her likely academic achievements at Key Stage 4.

- *Option 2.* Accept that Key Stage 4 is not for all pupils (some simply do not want to continue in a school environment). Support alternatives such as courses which bridge school and the world of work, or offer more vocational college-based courses, or disapply the National Curriculum and increase the level of work experience. Some examples of existing programmes are given in Appendix 3.

High-risk factors for potential school failure

Goodchild and Williams (1994) reported two main factors contributing to exclusion: events leading to uncertainties in life (such as arguments or family breakdown) and bullying in school (which they take in the widest sense to include verbal bullying, and bullying by adults). As they say:

> *Behaviour problems at home and school were seen as symptomatic of stress and should not have been a cause for exclusion.*

On the other hand, Carol Hayden (1994) provides some graphic descriptions of the kinds of pressure placed on teachers and classmates by difficult children. She gives this example of a woman quoted in a police report:

> *'She said … a ten-year-old boy brandishing a knife was almost certainly her son. She was at her wits' end and couldn't control him.'*

However, the report continues:

> *'… Mrs Bates has a full-time job and cannot supervise Geoff throughout the day. … he hasn't attended school for the past two years.'* (p. 265)

No evidence was reported by Hayden of any effective action by relevant agencies throughout this time. Many mothers go to work, but their children do not brandish knives at school. The important distinctions are in the way Mrs Bates constructs her life and manages her responsibilities, not in the social group to which she may be assigned by virtue of her income or her locality. One key aspect of this is whether she has any help to do so successfully, either from professionals or her personal network. Inadequacy, like exclusion, is a socially mediated construct – in other words, whether we prove to be inadequate depends on the number and scale of our daily tasks, and the amount of assistance we receive.

One way around the problem of lack of data about the underlying causes of school exclusion and effective responses is to turn to studies of youth crime and probationary work. This is a pragmatic step designed to allow for a broader understanding of possible causes, and not an acceptance of the 'delinquent' view of exclusion. Regardless of one's philosophical and political stance, the functional meaning of exclusion is that it is a punishment for misdemeanours. Furthermore, as things stand, school failure and dropout, or exclusion, does often lead on to juvenile crime, as in a self-fulfilling prophesy, and so the antecedents are logically likely to be the same.

Numerous significant risk factors have been found to predict offending and antisocial behaviour, often depending on the focus of the researcher. Farrington (1996) combined these under four headings (largely confirmed by OfSTED research): low attainment in school; inadequate parenting; impulsivity; and poverty.

- *Low attainment in school.* This can result from low intelligence, poor attendance, sickness in school, specific learning difficulties, inadequate or interrupted schooling, and negative life-events such as bereavement or parental redundancy, or chronic disadvantageous circumstances such as parental mental or physical illness, and the well-recognised educational factors such as poor acquisition of basic skills, particularly literacy.

- *Inadequate parenting.* This may also relate to a host of other factors, such as the use of harsh and excessive discipline, poor supervision, parental conflict, inexperienced or immature parents, confused and inconsistent management, cruel, passive or neglecting parental attitudes which fail to provide security of attachment, lack of interest in their child's development, family criminality, delinquent older siblings, and parental mental or physical illness. Security of attachment (from which comes a sense of self-worth and identity through which self-understanding and understanding of others can develop) is often weak.

- *Impulsivity.* Offenders frequently appear to have difficulty in thinking abstractly rather than concretely, for instance about the likely consequences of their actions. They are unlikely to have considered how their behaviour will affect their victims, and instead are egocentric.

- *Poverty.* Family poverty was characterised by low incomes, large family size, and poor housing, chronic or regular unemployment.

Many of the factors Farrington identifies are relevant to schooling as well as offending behaviour in later life. In fact a number of the school-based predictors he identifies would also be seen by many school managers as problem behaviours which often lead to exclusion.

For instance:

- troublesomeness;
- dishonesty;
- daring;
- aggressiveness;
- poor concentration;
- restlessness;
- 'psychomotor impulsivity';
- low attainment in primary school;
- truanting.

Farrington's paper is worth reading carefully. He constructs a very clear picture of factors relevant to school exclusion. *However, it is possible to use this powerful analysis in a misguided way.* Firstly, any cumulative analysis will blur the significance of individual differences. In support of his analysis, Farrington rightly claims that his prediction scale, based on the factors already mentioned, is surprisingly accurate. Of the 55 boys scoring highest on the scale, 15 (27 per cent) became chronic offenders (compared with only 23 out of 411 boys – 6 per cent – in the whole sample). Thus the predictors obtained strong statistical support. But what of the 40 high-scoring boys (73 per cent) who did not offend at all? Clearly there are other factors involved, *which are perhaps much harder to quantify.* Secondly, there are numerous opportunities for professionals involved with the child and the family (in particular the social agencies) to intervene, and so these factors should not be seen in isolation. These children grow up within a social environment which extends beyond the immediate family. Parents are also engaged in a process of lifelong learning and development, and this too is amenable to intervention from the community.

Graham (1988) found that high levels of mistrust between teachers and pupils, a lack of commitment to the school, and inconsistent or unclear rules all contributed to a higher level of delinquency. It is more difficult to say which factors are dependent (i.e. are consequences) and which are truly causal. In this case, as Graham acknowledges, it is difficult to say which comes first, the delinquent behaviour of the pupils, the background from which they come, or the poor school ethos.

Blyth and Milner (1993) see school exclusion as part of a process of civic exclusion, which develops through the operation of a 'constellation of disadvantage and inequality'. If schools see themselves as part of the community then they are likely to have a more inclusive attitude to difficult pupils. The territorial instincts of some school professionals and managers is a hindrance to the development of a good and inclusive ethos because such entrenched attitudes encourage the view that the school is a fortress beleaguered by an inimical society.

This appears to be recognized by some western countries, and as Parfrey (1997) says:

> 'Exclusion, it seems, is a matter of attitudes. ... Some countries see exclusion as a denial of human rights and do not allow schools to exclude any child. Canada, for instance, and the USA.' (p. 119)

Excluded families

It will come as no surprise to teachers to hear that families influence school behaviour. The difficulty for schools is to do anything about this, within their limited resources, and sphere of expertise. A Joseph Rowntree Foundation report in 1994 suggested that intervention was needed for families as well as for schools, but did not say how that was to be achieved.

Communication between families and school can sometimes be an artificial experience, probably because, in order to meet, both must function outside their normal orbits of activity. Schools set up meetings at which educational information is summarised in a way that gives the parent a selective view of the school's concerns and which may bear little relation to the parent's understanding of school or their child. Parents respond in an equally transparent way, whilst saving their real response (the one which would provide insight into their role) for home. This is not always the case, and intervention by the school directed towards families, where it is part of genuine efforts to divert the pupil, can be successful.

Pupils are much less likely to fail when a real and continuing bond has been established between family and school. This bond will almost always rely upon a 'special' person-to-person relationship.

This relationship could be between class teacher and father, head teacher and mother, or any other combination – such as an SEN Co-ordinator (SENCo) who forms a close link to the pupil's adult sister. The importance of establishing this special link is often in inverse proportion to the families' ability to do so successfully. Difficult children may have, for instance, a mother who is single, without a car, holding down a job she is worried about losing, who has younger children to collect and care for after school, with very little support. How can this mother fit into the class teacher's own busy schedule and get to the meeting or succession of meetings offered by the school? If she does not even have the bus fare to get to the school (this does happen), which option would you suggest she takes: make up a story, just not turn up, or be obliged to tell the school secretary or someone else she does not know that she is bone-poor? What about *her* self-esteem?

Vulnerable families have difficulty responding constructively to stress. Vulnerability factors may include:

- being a single parent, especially in the absence of a support network;

- being poor;

- encountering cultural barriers, especially involving language;

- mental health difficulties;

- one or both parents having a history of special needs;

- one or both parents having been excluded from school.

Destructive families, consciously or unconsciously, sabotage efforts by the school and the pupil to succeed. This often results from misguided efforts to back the pupil when in trouble. Destructive parents may:

- fail to give moral support to their child;

- fail to encourage the child to apologise or redress the situation;

- side with the pupil, while knowing that he or she is in the wrong;

- convey their own low opinion of teachers and school to the child;

- instruct their child to blatantly challenge the authority of the staff;

- give very unwise general advice, such as 'You don't have to do anything you don't want to'.

Additionally, they may establish a consistently negative role-model, or pre-emptively act to alter the situation for the worse (for instance by removing their child from school temporarily or permanently).

Disturbed families are chaotic and confused. Where there are chronic violent arguments and domestic violence, alcoholism and drug abuse, or sexual, emotional or physical abuse of the child or the siblings, the pupil arrives at school inadequately prepared, distressed, tired and angry. Concern about family members, difficulty managing emotional reactions, and lack of inner emotional resources may create a situation where a pupil self-excludes in order to deal with matters outside school which seem more important; or the need to off-load may lead the pupil to act inappropriately with peers or staff.

Apparent behavioural difficulties are tagged 'disturbed behaviour', because teachers are at a loss to understand why the child has acted or over-reacted in this way. However, this behaviour has a rational explanation (often related to family events) which the child is unable or unwilling to explain, often because of guilt and shame.

Frequently, the parents of excluded children themselves had difficulties at school. They may have attended a special school, or have been permanently excluded from the mainstream. These parents transfer the disadvantage unwittingly to their children by modelling, and through their narratives of childhood anti-school behaviour. Even when alerted to this, the parents cannot switch to narrating positive experiences simply because they do not remember having had any! Pupils even reproduce the unconstructive approach to schools that their parents had had demonstrated to them by their grandparents, and sometimes intense feelings of anxiety or hostility towards schools are transferred in this way to the child.

Parents have on occasion admitted that they found it difficult to communicate with or visit their child's school because of this. One mother took her child away from a school because she had been recognised as an ex-pupil by a teacher who had been there for many years. Even though her son had not had any problems there she felt her own record would undermine him. Unwittingly she herself did just that, and he never settled in the new school, eventually being permanently excluded.

Families can be open, welcoming help; or they can be closed and self-protective. Parents may ask for and willingly adopt new strategies and approaches to caring for their children, or refuse to countenance change. *The school must work with parents, or despite them.* That is, where the parents are not able to contribute to the process of integration, the school will have to work with the pupil alone.

Part of the challenge of this work is to get alongside difficult people, win their trust and turn them. Sometimes people argue and reject what they are hearing, but later they think it through and move on.

By being scrupulously honest with oneself and the family, and promoting equity in the relationship, professionals take up a position of speaking with integrity and humility. Suggestions and insights are offered as *possibilities*, and families are *empowered to act*. The professional is acting as a catalyst, not an agent. The agents are the family members, and they must be encouraged to act, and not be de-skilled. In this sense the family are 'paraprofessionals', with their own culture which must be respected even (or perhaps especially) when its imperatives seem to conflict with our own.

4 Towards an inclusive culture in school

Both in policy-making and public discussion, the social exclusion of children from schools has only just begun to find a meaningful place. Although the problem is receiving far more sympathetic attention, there is still a substantial lack of consensus about how we should view the phenomenon, or what should be done about it, and not much published research describing which remedies work, and which do not.

Mainstream school reintegration of children with special needs became a *cause célèbre* of the 1990s. At its heart was the principle of inclusion. Proponents claimed the moral high ground, defending reintegration in terms of value to the community, equal opportunities, and equal access to the broad and full curriculum, and citing the inadequacy of segregated alternatives. Opponents claimed that funding and resources were inadequate, and that in practice the education of the many is diminished for the sake of the few.

Three groupings of children may be reintegrated – those with learning difficulties (LDs), those with physical difficulties (PDs) and those with behavioural difficulties (BDs). Children in the latter grouping, on the increase, are the principal subjects of this book, and their reintegration arouses the most opposition. In the four years from 1991 exclusions quadrupled though the numbers seem now to have stabilised, and even dropped slightly. Children in the LD and PD groupings have recognisable needs, requiring easily identified and workable planning and management solutions (e.g. differentiated education plans or building alterations). Potential benefits of extra school resources and raised social awareness are set against less time available for other children. But difficulties resulting in exclusion arise from complex combinations across the bio-psycho-social continuum of dysfunction, and through institutional incapability. Whilst education authorities and schools accept their responsibility to the wider community, often there are ambivalent feelings about children in the BD grouping, who pose problems that can confound even specialized institutions. They are not seen as 'disabled' but as a source of stress in teachers and fear in other children: causes, problems and solutions are all contentious. An excluded child comes into direct contact with local authority systems, returning to school or into segregated provision within an obligatory statutory framework, but for many there has been little professional help or social/educational input.

The underlying principles of inclusion reflect a growing consensus, the beginnings of which could be seen in the Education Act 1981. This act required maintained schools to use their best endeavours to make provision for SEN pupils, and gave parents a right of appeal against decisions affecting their child. The Children Act 1989, described by the then Lord Chancellor as 'the most far-reaching reform of child care law ... in living memory', extended the principle of self-advocacy to children and families. New advice was issued to social services offices through the 'Orange Book' on the assessment of children, which acknowledged that institutions had inherent weaknesses, different from those presented by families, which could place a child at risk. The Education Act 1993, from which stemmed the *Special Educational Needs Code of Practice* (SENCoP), followed a similar approach in ratifying a whole raft of key values:

- Partnerships between parents, children and the education service should be promoted.

- Continuity of need should be recognised.

- Specific educational and social needs should be met with specific provision.

- The effectiveness of that provision should be evaluated at all stages.

- Unreasonable delays in providing assessment and intervention should be avoided.

- Education should take place within a mainstream setting wherever possible.

The genuine implementation of these principles for excluded children, rather than just for those whose special needs fit in with the *de facto* perspective of the teaching profession, is for many people a step too far. The provision of effective programmes to meet the needs of excluded children is a step towards equality of opportunity for a disadvantaged group. A number of studies (e.g. Brodie and Berridge, 1996) demonstrate that there are a disproportionate number of African–Caribbean pupils amongst excludees. This systematic bias is relatively easy to identify, but there is also an unsystematic bias against a diverse group of pupils, including those whose carers have mental health problems, or who have suffered bereavement or other losses, and those with non-specific and unrecognised learning difficulties, and many others with generalised problems. The world is full of marginalised people, whose children become marginalised too.

▰ The principled perspective

Five overarching principles need to be upheld by everyone involved in making decisions about children at risk of school failure.

▰ First principle: Natural justice demands equality of opportunity

There is plenty of evidence that a disproportionate number of African–Caribbean children are being excluded. Children in care are also up to ten times more likely to be excluded. There are regional variations which fly in the face of common sense – for instance, no children in Glasgow were permanently excluded in 1996/97. Presumably this is not a result of the legendary good behaviour of young Glaswegians! Pupils in England are more than eight times more likely to be excluded than pupils in Northern Ireland, and four times more likely than pupils in Scotland.

There are plenty of other ways in which the process of exclusion fails to meet criteria for equal opportunities. There may be inconsistency in responding to misdemeanours (both between schools and between pupils), the frequent absence of a fair hearing, and the likelihood that factors outside the school's boundary may be overlooked. Different teachers appear to have very different experiences with the same pupils, and problem children are frequently expelled from classes where there is an obvious lack of control and direction.

In 1999 Lord Macpherson produced his report into the murder of Stephen Lawrence, and its publication triggered some excitement in the media as to the possible existence of institutional racism in cultures other than the police force. The report presents something of a challenge to us all. Some might suggest that the data on exclusions speaks for itself. Teachers' unions, however, were quick (in fact, too quick) to jump to their members' defence. The key word inserted by Macpherson is 'unwitting'. It is worth quoting word for word from the report since his position may all too easily be misrepresented.

Stephen Lawrence, a black youth, was murdered in a wanton act of violence on the streets of South London in April 1993, allegedly by a group of white youths. The behaviour of the police both at the time (their initial reaction was to arrest Stephen's friend), and later on in the pursuit of the murder investigations, led to the setting up of Macpherson's review. Here are some excerpts from the report:

> Each of 17 officers interviewed ... was baldly asked whether his or her 'judgment and subsequent actions were based on the fact that Stephen was black'. In some cases Mrs Lawrence's condemnatory words about the lack of first-aid were quoted to the officers. Each officer roundly denied racism or racist conduct. Each officer plainly and genuinely believed that he or she had acted without overt racist bias or discrimination. The answers given were thus predictable ... The suggestion being made is that practices may be adopted by public bodies as well as private individuals which are unwittingly discriminatory against black people ... this is an allegation which deserves serious consideration, and, where proved, swift remedy. ... In 1981 Lord Scarman's report into the Brixton Disorders was presented to Parliament. In that seminal report Lord Scarman responded to the suggestion that Britain is an institutionally racist society in this way: 'If, by [institutionally racist] it is meant that [Britain] is a society which knowingly, as a matter of policy, discriminates against black people, I reject the allegation.' ... Unwitting racism can arise because of lack of understanding, ignorance or mistaken beliefs. It can arise from well-intentioned but patronising words or actions. It can arise from unfamiliarity with the behaviour or cultural traditions of people or families from minority ethnic communities. It can arise from racist stereotyping of black people as potential criminals or troublemakers. Often this arises out of uncritical self-understanding born out of an inflexible police ethos of the 'traditional' way of doing things. Furthermore such attitudes can thrive in a tightly knit community, so that there can be a collective failure to detect and to outlaw this breed of racism.

The following three vignettes are examples of what I believe Macpherson would call unwitting racism. Whilst they are relatively innocuous they do effectively show how the assumptions are there, just below the surface, and how they can emerge to distort practice. The first two, especially, reflect a fall into 'the stereotype trap' by making assumptions that were literally pre-judicial. The third has a more insidious tone. Sceptics may doubt the veracity of this narrative. It was reported first-hand by an A-level pupil who gave every indication of being truthful, and who had a first-class school record.

Vignette 1

One girl at school in Year 9 heard an announcement that she should attend extra English classes after school. But her English was perfectly good. She saw this as a kind of punishment. When she told her father that the only reason she was being told to attend was because she was of foreign origin, her father was angry and would not let her go. Some teachers later complained that they had tried to provide extra help for those who needed it but they didn't bother to turn up!

Vignette 2

An Arab pupil in Year 8 received a phone call from her tutor:

> *'Your father said he could not come to the options meeting tomorrow at six o'clock. I can't offer him any other time.'*

> *'Hang on, I'll get my mother.'*

> *'Well can you explain it to her for me?'*

> *'My mother speaks perfect English, you know.'*

The father later complained that he should have been offered an alternative time – he was working at six o'clock.

Vignette 3

At an A level parents' evening, the media studies teacher told an Algerian pupil's mother that the price of a book her son needed was £15.99. When she showed some anxiety at the price, the teacher asked her: 'Can't your husband get a second job?'

One final quote from the Macpherson report is irresistible:

> *Sir Henry Brooke's perceptive 1993 Kapila Lecture should be required reading in the field of race relations. He reminded us that in the 1st Century AD Philo wrote 'When a judge tries a case he must remember that he is himself on trial.'*

Every head teacher who considers a pupil's actions in relation to reported misbehaviour is acting as a judge. Serious sanctions such as exclusion have a quasi-legal impact. Senior managers will want to ensure that questions of fairness are uppermost in the minds of all concerned.

▓▓▓▓ Second principle: Effective action is innovative action

Difficult children are demanding. Their problems do seem insurmountable, and plans made are likely to fail. A typical response to the failure of a plan is to say 'This pupil is worse than we thought.' In other words, instead of throwing the plan out, we will throw the pupil out!

It must be remembered that each pupil is distinct and individual. The school will need to search for innovative ways to approach assessment and planning for intervention. This is not as difficult as it seems. There is a similar difference between a musician playing from sheet music and one who is using well-rehearsed harmony and technique to extemporise.

▪ Third principle: Inclusive education depends on an inclusive ethos

Inclusion is not something that just happens. The dynamic of exclusion is deeply ingrained in the human psyche, just as racism is. Both arise from the *xenophobic impulse* which was originally a protective factor in social groups. Historically, where different troupes, herds, packs or tribes competed for territory and resources, the ability to recognise an individual as from another tribe (and therefore dangerous), to feel fear and aversion, and to flee promptly or drive that individual away, was a life-protecting attribute. This is the origin of xenophobia, and it is still in us today. Like many primeval urges it needs to be controlled; but first it needs to be recognised.

Recent events in the former Yugoslavia are a reminder that the fabric of social cohesion – even in countries that are supposed to be 'developed' and 'modern' – is frighteningly thin. Many people believe that some of our fellow countrymen, if invited to do so by the authorities, would jump at the chance to behave in the cruel and degrading way revealed to us by the media in Bosnia, Kosovo and elsewhere. Indeed, few have the strength or courage to resist the force of group expectation.

The selective rejection of individuals from the group is seen in animals and humans, both now and throughout history. They become marked out by their differences as dangerous to the social order and deserving of expulsion from society. Where individuals have different social or cultural expressions, this can be, and frequently is, interpreted as deviant. Social cohesion with any social group is maintained by demarcating the boundary between those who are in the group and those who are outside. Any minority group may be excluded by the xenophobic fears of the majority. This exclusion is always rationally justified on grounds of the social health and wellbeing of both the majority and the minority, and perceptions are filtered to support this view.

Against this is set the enlightened view – that inclusion is a healthier and altogether more positive option. It is the courageous approach, stemming from the confident and expansive appreciation of the value of others. Inclusion is more idealistic, a celebration of diversity. It is an expression of a shared humanity, of the need for community and mutual support. It is the mark of a society that can afford to care and chooses to do so.

It is just necessary to bear in mind that the 'shadowy reactionary forces' are also at work. A school needs to work consciously towards an *inclusive ethos*, and formally uphold the progressive outlook described above. A contemporary test of this might be the way each school and authority reacts to the 'Macpherson' challenge described above. Is there an angry rejection of his concerns: 'How dare anyone suggest that our schools and our teachers (who are apparently above all reproach) might need to reconsider how well they understand children from a diversity of racial and ethnic backgrounds!' Or is there a more accommodating reflective response: 'Yes, we can see the value of looking again at how we can bring families, pupils and schools closer together in mutual appreciation of our different perspectives.'

▓▓▓ Fourth principle: An inside perspective is needed to engineer real change

Where there is a substantial gulf in perception of a problem, there is seldom agreement about the solution. One characteristic of children at risk of school failure is that the perceptions of school, home and pupil are so different (see Figure 6). This difference can be found between the school's staff, too, and disruptive children can split a staffroom down the middle.

Hassan was an interesting and serious case, and the request for a statement of special needs made shortly before his permanent exclusion was accompanied by a large and truly dreadful account of his behaviour. The management of his case is described in Appendix 1. Although Hassan and his family were known to social services and the family guidance service for a considerable time, they did not appear to have uncovered, or considered significant, the inside perspectives briefly summarised in the third section of Figure 6. The successful outcome to this case was achieved largely by the efforts of family members, with facilitation from outreach workers.

Here is an excerpt from a negative written pupil referral for a boy called Chico:

> *Chico would not settle down at the beginning of class and open his book. I asked him again and again but he still did nothing. He was distracting the other pupils. He started to argue when I spoke to him, and refused to go to the withdrawal room when asked to do so. I called the Head of Year and he took him out of class.*

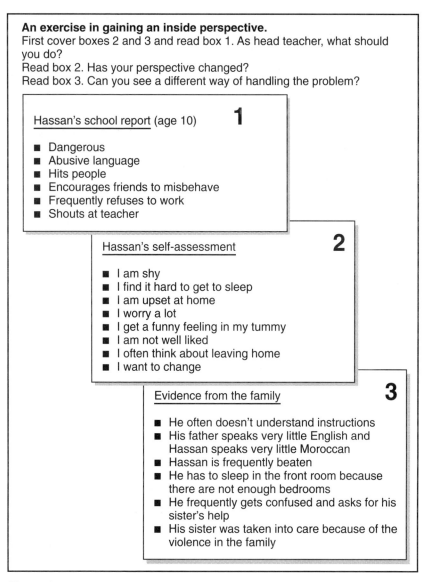

An exercise in gaining an inside perspective.
First cover boxes 2 and 3 and read box 1. As head teacher, what should you do?
Read box 2. Has your perspective changed?
Read box 3. Can you see a different way of handling the problem?

Hassan's school report (age 10)   **1**

- Dangerous
- Abusive language
- Hits people
- Encourages friends to misbehave
- Frequently refuses to work
- Shouts at teacher

Hassan's self-assessment   **2**

- I am shy
- I find it hard to get to sleep
- I am upset at home
- I worry a lot
- I get a funny feeling in my tummy
- I am not well liked
- I often think about leaving home
- I want to change

Evidence from the family   **3**

- He often doesn't understand instructions
- His father speaks very little English and Hassan speaks very little Moroccan
- Hassan is frequently beaten
- He has to sleep in the front room because there are not enough bedrooms
- He frequently gets confused and asks for his sister's help
- His sister was taken into care because of the violence in the family

Figure 6

Here is what the same teacher said, when given an opportunity to speak in confidence about Chico:

> *He drives me mad. I feel myself being drawn into this role of the 'bitchy teacher'. I try to stop myself, but in the end I cannot. It's as if he wants to force me to do this. One time I gave him a real dressing down and he went all*

*quiet and got on with his work. I could see his feelings were hurt, and it made
me feel so guilty.*

The inside perspective of the teacher revealed her deep insecurities about
her class management style, both in terms of control and in creating the
'right' ambience. Once the inside perspective of the pupil himself was
shared with her (through the mediation of a pupil advocate), she was
able to review the way she used her long experience and teaching skills,
without the need to exclude him.

Fifth principle: Intervention must be structured

If change is what is required, then the outreach worker is involved in the
'management of change'. McCalman and Patton, in their book *Change
Management: A Guide to Effective Implementation*, identify two kinds of
change – soft and hard.

Change is always almost always both 'soft' and 'hard'. But in seeking
to turn a pupil away from school failure, it is clear that a largely soft
change is required. This is why there is so much emphasis in this book

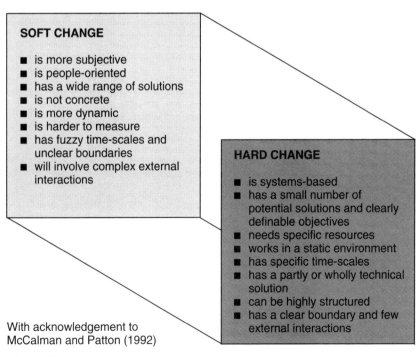

SOFT CHANGE

- is more subjective
- is people-oriented
- has a wide range of solutions
- is not concrete
- is more dynamic
- is harder to measure
- has fuzzy time-scales and
  unclear boundaries
- will involve complex external
  interactions

HARD CHANGE

- is systems-based
- has a small number of
  potential solutions and clearly
  definable objectives
- needs specific resources
- works in a static environment
- has specific time-scales
- has a partly or wholly technical
  solution
- can be highly structured
- has a clear boundary and few
  external interactions

With acknowledgement to
McCalman and Patton (1992)

Figure 7

on style, approach, awareness and sensitivity. It also explains why categorical, technical and systems-based approaches so often have little impact on the problem.

A consultant was asked recently to try to prevent the permanent exclusion of Michael, a pupil who was 'teetering on the brink'. Negative referrals had piled up which described him (in terms) as an attention-seeking, argumentative smart-alec. The young man was becoming more and more marginalized, and in fact was already internally excluded from the tutor group. The consultant took him to a local hamburger bar and invited him to choose whatever he wanted off the menu. From his reaction it appeared that treats were a rare event in his life. Away from his peers and in a slightly unusual social setting his real nature asserted itself – anxious, uncertain and depressed. Nobody loved him, he didn't think he had any friends, the teachers were too hard on him, and so on. A meeting with mother (in the staff canteen at her place of work) led to further disclosures. His father had recently been released from prison on charges relating to the physical abuse of women, but Michael did not want to stay with him, because the violence was continuing with the father's new partner. There were few male role-models in Michael's life and his mother with a younger daughter to care for, and a job to hold down, had little time to spare for her son.

The consultant helped the mother to identify a male relation who did visit from time to time and she agreed to talk to him about making a point of supporting her son. Michael was persuaded that the teachers did care about him and that they were going to try to support him more. He was encouraged to try again to meet the teachers half-way. The main thing, however, was that the teachers were given a chance to talk about Michael with the consultant on a one-to-one basis. Their concerns were respected and acknowledged, but in return the consultant described to them a very different boy – Michael in reality, or at least the version found under the phony aggressive exterior. They were then able to join up some previously overlooked pieces of their own 'jigsaw' and started to respond to him differently. Informal feedback a while later showed that, although Michael's behaviour had only changed slightly, the reasons teachers put forward were quite different. Later, the head teacher told me that Michael was no longer 'on the hit list', not because his behaviour was so much better, but because those pushing the head-of-year to agitate for his exclusion were no longer doing so.

This is what is meant by soft change. The attitudes and awareness of the teachers and the pupil had been altered. Over a period of time, one would expect that Michael really would develop a new school 'identity' which was more realistic and manageable.

However, soft change must still be structured, and indeed this is an essential prerequisite for balancing the 'softness' of the intervention. Change that is wholly soft is difficult to measure, difficult to validate and hard to maintain. Some examples of unstructured soft-change strategies that are unlikely to be very effective might be:

1. asking a pupil to try harder;

2. asking staff to be more sympathetic;

3. writing a plan which calls for 'raising self-esteem'.

Those same examples become structured as follows:

1. Ask staff to find ways to give 'approval' to the pupil by making a point of speaking to him when he comes in the room, inviting him to sit at the front, and encouraging him to work with a pupil who is new to the class.

2. Visit the home, on several occasions, and listen to the mother. Find ways to enable him to get more sleep, and leave for school in a more optimistic frame of mind. At school, make sure teachers know that his reading is adequate but very slow, and that he should have time to read instructions without being shown up, or alternatively ask someone to help him with this discreetly.

3. Find out whether he has any special abilities or secret ambitions – perhaps to lift weights or join a football team. Help him to get involved in something which makes him feel good about himself.

'Structured' interventions are:

- principled;

- comprehensive;

- well organised;

- carefully staged;

- reviewed and modified;

- delivered by 100 per cent commitment to the change objectives.

A whole-school approach to inclusion

Schools can do a great deal, without additional resources, to reduce exclusions by:

■ adopting unambiguous rules;

■ having a clear hierarchy of sanctions;

■ applying rules consistently;

■ ensuring pupils know the consequences of their behaviour;

■ involving parents much sooner;

■ trying mediation instead of confrontation;

■ thinking therapeutically rather than punitively.

'Unambiguous rules' and 'therapeutic thinking' are not at odds with one another. Pupils will respond much better to rules and boundaries if they are seen not as a control tool manipulated by teachers, but as a system within which both are required to operate. After all, staff are also keeping the rules (or they should be). In fact, pupils and teachers are on the same side!

In addition the following measures can also reduce exclusion rates, but each has a resource and planning implication:

■ The education system as a whole needs to pick up problems much earlier.

■ There needs to be improved training for all staff.

■ Improved community links can support children from particular minority cultures and provide mentors and role models for children at risk of failure.

■ Adapt the curriculum, particularly for older children.

■ Get others involved in the process of advocacy, mediation and intervention – professional bodies, statutory and voluntary agencies and especially parents.

If you must exclude, do so internally, perhaps for part of the school day or a particular lesson. This means that pupils are not out on a limb, at risk of learning more delinquency skills; and it ensures they are maintaining their school attendance habits. The government's Social Exclusion Unit suggests that groups of schools could work together to run informal 'one in – one out' arrangements for excluded children.

Thoughts on reintegration

Good public relations are a necessary part of successful reintegration work. Some key themes are as follows:

Excluded children are not delinquent and unpleasant thugs

This is too judgmental. These pupils are sadly misguided, vulnerable and confused. The idea that they have social disabilities needs to be promoted carefully in a way that gets the message across without arousing the anxieties of other disabled people, or a more general scepticism. We know they are socially disabled because they have poor inter- and intrapersonal skills. Put simply, if this were not so, they would never have self-injured themselves by getting excluded.

The 'threat' from reintegrated children needs to be kept in perspective

Permanent exclusion is a major and tragic problem for the pupils who have been excluded. But in practice, even under highly inclusive conditions, most classes would not have a single reintegrated child in them.

Many exclusions are at Key Stage 4

A different sort of provision is increasingly being made available. The remainder could be absorbed, if the professional consensus can be moved in the direction of inclusion with constraints.

Teacher expectations need to be appropriate

Reintegrated pupils will fall somewhere between the 'best' pupils and the 'worst'. So they should be treated like any other pupil in the school, including on disciplinary and behaviour matters. They should not be expected to be better than other pupils, and especially they should not feel that they are being scrutinised. In fact, they will need to be loved and tolerated for being awkward and eccentric characters.

Inclusion encourages a better school ethos

It will be better to manage pupils who need reintegrating into the heart of the school, and make sure they receive the help they need, with on-going support. The alternative scenario involves a culture of collusion, in which difficult children are scapegoated and punished, leaving their parents to find devious ways to gain their readmission without support, so that the school is without the benefit of a detailed knowledge of their background.

There is a continuing debate around inclusion and there are points to be made on both sides. *On the one hand*:

■ The needs of other children may be ignored.

■ 'Schools are for teaching children.'

- The problem lies beyond the school's control, and 'the government should do something about it'.

- Nobody, teachers or pupils, likes to be set up for failure.

- In-school programmes for dealing with a pupil at risk of failure have not worked.

- There is no culture of reintegration.

- Staff may be reluctant to put up with these 'pariahs', and reintegration is made harder by their resistance.

- The 'moral high ground' is inadequately resourced, and in practice the education of the many could be diminished for the sake of the few.

On the other hand:

- There's no such thing as exclusion! Excluded pupils can be moved only from one part of the community to another.

- In the excluding school, other pupils will quickly take their place as the 'focus of disaffection'.

- Failure is a partnership, too: schools, pupils, families and peer groups have all contributed to some extent.

- Special education is notoriously expensive! There is a clear social value resulting from an inclusion.

- The exclusion process is unsatisfactory and probably unconstitutional.

- Excluded pupils become parents of excluded children and perpetuate the cost to the next generation – our own children.

- Programmes of intervention can work.

- Teachers should not be expected to bear the responsibility for family and individual work. Schools should, however, be willing to work alongside other professionals who are tackling the problems beyond the school gate, and be sympathetic to the needs of returnees (see Figure 8).

Staff may have strong political objections to any reintegration, and an emotional resistance to returning pupils. This is based partly on a lack of information, and the stress created by displaced anxiety.

When one pupil was reintegrated into primary school, the class teacher insisted that a support teacher be there at all times. She was

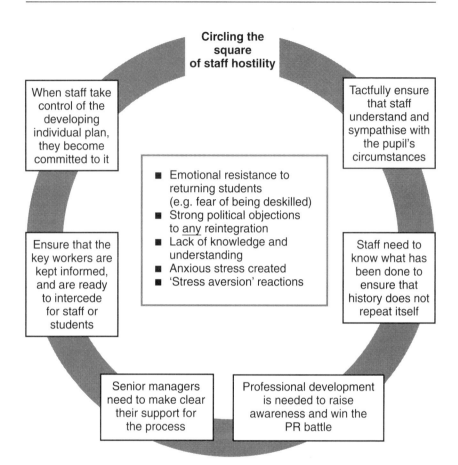

Circling the square of staff hostility

When staff take control of the developing individual plan, they become committed to it

Tactfully ensure that staff understand and sympathise with the pupil's circumstances

- Emotional resistance to returning students (e.g. fear of being deskilled)
- Strong political objections to <u>any</u> reintegration
- Lack of knowledge and understanding
- Anxious stress created
- 'Stress aversion' reactions

Ensure that the key workers are kept informed, and are ready to intercede for staff or students

Staff need to know what has been done to ensure that history does not repeat itself

Senior managers need to make clear their support for the process

Professional development is needed to raise awareness and win the PR battle

Figure 8

convinced that the moment she and the class were alone in the room with him, he would go berserk. Even after a week she was still convinced it was not safe, and kept him sitting apart from the others.

■ Steps to improve the chances of successful reintegration

First, make sure staff take control of the developing individual plan. People who are involved in managing change have a way of becoming committed to its success. This reintegration is not like others – it has been managed, and real intervention has taken place. One essential element must be in place – the determination of staff.

Second, the outreach worker needs to be kept informed, and be ready to intercede for staff or pupils. The outreach worker has everyone's ear, and vice versa. Problems, if they arise, can be quickly minimised provided they are made apparent.

Third, senior managers – without exception – need to make clear their support for the process. This is part of their commitment to the ethos of the school. It's just about leadership!

Fourth, professional development is needed to raise awareness and win the public-relations battle. Better trained staff will have a clearer understanding of the issues, more confidence in working at relationships, and more skills.

Fifth, staff need to know what has been done to ensure that history does not repeat itself. Belief in success is based on the idea that things are different this time.

Finally, staff must understand and sympathise with the pupil's circumstances. It is truly amazing how teachers' attitudes can change when they have some background knowledge, an 'inside perspective' on a pupil's troubles. Pupils who are lonely, anxious and depressed often appear in class as hostile, disruptive and work-shy. Usually teachers have no idea what is going on at home.

How views become fragmented

To some degree most people adapt their characteristics and behaviour for different contexts. We commonly describe this as 'taking on a role' – as a professional, as a partner in a relationship, as a parent, and in other social settings. Ideally, the different roles adopted form a harmonious *gestalt* (a unity which is greater than the sum of its parts), which constitutes a complete personality.

However, young lives are sometimes disrupted by badly managed family breakdown, and by excessive conflicting demands from families, peer groups, schools and media hype. They can also be distorted by dysfunctional relationships. When the competing demands of families, school society and inner need are too disparate, there comes a time when the young person can no longer fit the parts together. This does not mean the person is mentally ill, but mental health is compromised. This is well described by the word *fragmentation*. It is as if the young person uses one role or relationship to mitigate the residual stress of another.

One example of this is the phenomenon frequently observed by primary phase teachers that naughty children are sometimes reported by their parents as being as 'good as gold at home', and vice versa. This 'fragmentation' is part of normal development. It can be seen in young children, and from time to time in adolescence. Sometimes adolescents become very embarrassed by the presence of their parents at public events. This is because the emergent adult public persona they are carefully cultivating does not 'fit' with the childish state of being under a parent's wing whilst out and about.

For older pupils in difficulties at school, fragmentation increases and seems to spread outwards, manifesting in conflict between adults involved in their care in one way or another. Teachers will hold widely divergent views of a particular pupil's behaviour and its meaning, sometimes leading to highly charged disagreements at staff meetings. Psychologists submit reports that often seem wholly at variance with the experiences of those more closely involved who are often less qualified (but more experienced) staff. Families disagree amongst themselves about the best way forward, and efforts directed towards building satisfactory relationships between family and professionals seem to be sabotaged (always by the other side). Family/school communication becomes increasingly one-sided.

One obvious sign of this fragmentation is the variation in attitudes of teachers to pupils at risk. Some teachers have no difficulty with 'difficult' pupils, whilst others are brought to the point of breakdown and demand 'action' from senior managers. As the situation deteriorates, some staff members and the family can become increasingly defensive in the maintenance of their positions – misunderstandings occur, tempers become frayed, and the stress level goes on increasing.

The distinction some over-emotional teachers fail to make is that it is often their perceptions that catalyse the kinds of interaction leading to conflict, and then punishment and isolation, for such individuals. Such teachers are driven by their need to find a scapegoat for unexpressed feelings of failure, and challenges to their competence, sense of self-worth or identity.

Understanding the exclusion culture

Readers will already be aware that there is a good deal of 'psychology' in the approach taken by this book. In psychological terms, 'power' is just one dimension within a relationship. In legal terms, parents and children are seen as having very different rights and responsibilities. In psychological terms, though one is more powerful than the other, the parent and child are simply two personas or identities within a social context. Neither has primacy over the other – that is, the parent's authority is simply another element in the psychological construction. The same applies to a psychological interpretation of school-based dynamics.

What follows here is a psychological interpretation of the phenomenon of exclusion. *It is not the only construction which can be made of events, but it is one that is often overlooked and needs to be acknowledged.*

It is not intended to suggest that all schools function in the same way. There are many good schools, an abundance of good practice, and numerous dedicated teachers to whom their pupils owe a great deal. Many pupils pass their school life without noticeable difficulty. Where there are problems, schools often handle them well. But it would be foolish to deny that in some schools this is not the case. Even in good schools, it is not always the case.

In order to claim that the exclusion of any pupil was justified absolutely, one would first have to show that no alternatives could have succeeded. The best that any school can claim is that no alternatives *that seemed to be available at the time* could have succeeded. In order to extend and improve on those alternatives it is worth taking an honest and frank look at the mechanisms of exclusion.

A fixed-term exclusion sets a dangerous precedent. It is a high-risk strategy, which may produce changes in behaviour in some cases. We do not know, for sure, how many. The problem is that if it does not work, it simply sets in motion a downward momentum towards longer term and (eventually) permanent exclusion. Unfortunately, exclusion will fail to modify the behaviour of just that group of pupils who most need real help – the ones who cannot help themselves. As pointed out elsewhere, fixed-term exclusion could be used as part of a structured intervention to provide respite and an opportunity to tackle the pupil's problems.

The DfEE's guidance document *Social Inclusion: Pupil Support* (1999) did not greatly change the codes for fixed-term exclusions. There are the three criteria:

- that there has been serious breach of the school's discipline policy;
- a range of alternative stategies has been tried;
- allowing the pupil to stay at school would seriously harm the education or welfare of the pupil or other children.

Some further advice is provided which elaborates on each criterion, and there are some unacceptable reasons for exclusion: it should not be used for failure to do homework or bring dinner money, for poor academic performance, for lateness, truancy, wrong clothing or hairstyle, or for parental behaviour. There is also a requirement that in the case of longer term-fixed exclusions (more than 15 days) the school must have a plan that will (a) enable the pupil to continue his or her education, (b) address the pupil's problems, and (c) provide for reintegration into the school.

However, the guidance is to some extent an armchair lawyer's charter. What is meant by 'seriously harm the education of the pupil or other child'? Legal experts will tell you that this sort of clause lines lawyers' pockets. However, as I discuss in more detail in Chapter 4, the exclusion process is quasi-legal but lacks jurisprudence (the protocols of law in action, from *habeus corpus* to the installation of a jury). In effect, as long as the reason is not one of the unacceptable criteria mentioned in the paragraph above, a child can be excluded. In any event, the process of appeal (which can usually be organised only for a date after the exclusion has been completed) or reinstatement is so ponderous and difficult for parents that little redresss is possible.

Here are some alternative guidelines:

- A pupil may be excluded for a very short time in order to allow parents to be contacted and an outreach worker to set up an informal meeting.

- A pupil may be excluded for a longer (fixed) term when the pupil would benefit from a period of respite from school, provided specific plans for assessment and intervention to address the pupil's needs are in place.

- A pupil may be excluded – for as short a period as possible – if he or she represents a real and immediate threat to the welfare of other children and plans are in place to hold a meeting with the pupil and other pupil representatives to discuss how the situation can be defused. In this case, the pupil concerned and those most likely to be threatened should have peer and adult supporters who will help them negotiate a working solution to the problems.

Fixed terms should *never* be applied:

- where the current (1999) DfEE guidance precludes it;

- on a tariff basis (such as one day for a first offence of swearing at teacher, three days for a second offence; one day for bullying; etc.);

- as retribution, punishment or 'as an example to others';

- in the absence of *proactive* plans for the management of the period of exclusion, however short.

Permanent exclusion should be used *only* if a pupil's behaviour would be considered criminal under the law, and is sufficiently serious to warrant prosecution, or would have been if the pupil was over 16. In this case the local education authority should take immediate steps to provide an alternative place of education or a place at an authorised young person's support centre (such as a Pupil Referral Unit).

The failure which exclusion represents for all parties generates a high level of guilt and consequent denial. Readers may view some of what follows sceptically, especially if they assume that professionals are always 'professional'. They should be reassured that the processes described below really do occur. It may also appear to suggest that the schools are always at fault, which is not the case. Wherever the fault lies, however, the school is always the strongest party. This means schools must seek to take responsibility for finding solutions, even when the problems originate elsewhere.

▆ Examining pathways

In critical situations differing imperatives and contexts create markedly different perceptions, driving the various characters in the drama to act out what seem to be irresistible roles. On those occasions where individual members of staff have acted unreasonably or incompetently so as to increase the likelihood of a pupil being at risk of school failure, such actions would be readily apparent to any observer. The purpose of what follows is not, therefore, to apportion blame, but to raise awareness of the hidden mechanisms which result in the violation of the school's stated aims and ethos, in spite of what appears to be everyone's best efforts.

Most professionals are aware of the dynamics which are described here. The problem is how to intervene so as to change them without demoralising teachers who are already struggling to cope, and feeling insecure about their role.

Pupils at risk of school failure draw attention to themselves. Their behaviour in class is:

- off-task;

- disruptive of class teaching;

- disturbing to other pupils;

- conflicting with peers;

- confrontational with the teacher, especially around discipline and class management.

Outside class their behaviour is 'antisocial', leading to complaints to staff by other pupils or by staff themselves. There may also be serious 'incidents' either in or out of school.

These pupils eventually enter a process within which a number of distinct but interwoven pathways to failure are followed. Which pathways predominate will depend on the school and its staff. Some pathways are formal, others informal. Most are overt, but the key process of social exclusion is both informal and covert.

Pathway 1: 'Let the punishment fit the crime'

Pupils who regularly come to the attention of the senior management for unsatisfactory behaviour will become involved with the formal disciplinary procedures of the school, encapsulated in the school's 'behaviour management policy'. These reflect, and are supported by, various DfEE circulars. The policy will set down a framework of sanctions, including detention, withdrawal room and fixed-term exclusions tariffs, which ultimately lead to permanent exclusion. A very few schools have a no-exclusions policy, generally relying on alternative strategies in conjunction with local schools' compacts and the local education authority. Parents of excluded pupils have a right of appeal, and so the school must be able to provide 'evidence' that the exclusion is justified. The collection of this evidence is time-consuming and seldom in the pupil's best interests.

Serious incidents will result in a pupil jumping directly to a higher level in the process – permanent exclusion can be summary and immediate following a single offence (in many schools, for instance, for carrying a knife or other weapon). Generally however, the behaviour management policy includes many checks and balances, which appear to allow pupils ample opportunity to alter behaviour. The policy safeguards the authority of the school, and the power of the governing body. Although it may be more or less systematically applied, schools invariably have some sort of structured procedures in place (even if this is only custom and practice based on what the head teacher usually does). However, it does not in itself contain any remedial mechanism, being quasi-legal and therefore, to paraphrase George Chapman (1559–1634), a sort of ass.

Pathway 2: 'A code without a practice'

This second track involves implementation of the *Special Educational Needs Code of Practice* (SENCoP 1994). There are five stages to this process. From stage one the pupil must to be placed on a register of special needs, and parents informed and involved in decision-making and, hopefully, effective action.

1. The class tutor formally implements an 'individual education plan'.

2. If that does not solve the problem, the SEN Co-ordinator (SENCo) is involved in setting up a wider-ranging individual plan.

3. If that does not solve the problem, external agencies become involved in a third level of intervention.

4. If that does not solve the problem, a Statement of Special Needs is applied for, requiring a formal multi-agency assessment.

5. If the assessment identifies enduring special needs then a Statement of Special Needs is drafted and generally approved, or otherwise a 'note in lieu' is issued.

The Statement, which is a closely circumscribed legal document, can specify support in the mainstream, a special school or occasionally some other specific provision. However, such resources have to come from within the local authority's fixed budget, and so a very difficult balance must be struck between needs and resources. There is an inevitable conflict of interests. It has been said that all children have their own special needs. How true, and how impossible!

The whole process through stages 1 to 5 will generally take at least a year (for instance, the *Code of Practice* sets an upper limit of six months for stage 4 alone). Schools should be able to justify each move between stages by showing that less substantial actions have failed to alleviate the problem over a reasonable period of time. The SEN process and the behaviour management policy of a school operate independently, and a pupil can be excluded at any stage of the SENCoP process.

The *Code of Practice*, where it is properly applied, is a fair approach to children who present special difficulties, although a more flexible and less bureaucratic framework would be a positive development. However, schools frequently do not implement this option for children who show difficult behaviour, perhaps because the problems are usually acute and immediate action seems more appropriate; and also perhaps because behavioural difficulties are not perceived as a disability in the way learning difficulties are, and hence pupils with behavioural difficulties 'do not deserve' (as teachers have been heard to say) the extra effort and resources involved in developing, implementing and reviewing an individual plan. Consequently, pupils with behavioural difficulties are hardly ever assessed as having special needs, leading to a Statement which would result in their removal from, or support in, a mainstream school without being permanently excluded first.

▓▓▓ Pathway 3: 'Make or break strategies'

Many schools do initiate formal and systematic approaches to dealing with difficult children, which often parallel the *Code of Practice*, inasmuch as a structured and specific individual plan is developed which involves an increasingly wide circle of professionals. These can be effective in diverting many children away from failure. There is not room in this account to describe all the examples of good practice within and without schools and community networks, which are delivering the kind of programme described here for pupils who are experiencing difficulties in school (for further information see Appendix 3).

Frequently, senior staff or tutors make genuine efforts, on an informal basis, to try to divert the pupil away from a crisis. For instance:

- making and taking time to talk one-to-one to the pupil's own agenda;

- contacting and sharing concerns with families in a no-blame, collaborative way;

- finding practical ways to alter the circumstances underpinning the pupil's difficulties.

McLean (1997) suggests that these kinds of initiative are the key to successful preventative work. There are three good reasons why these approaches break down:

- Sometimes the circumstances behind the exclusion are simply beyond the school's circle of influence.

- The professionals concerned seldom feel able to tackle the relationship factors between 'problem' children and 'problem' staff.

- Whether, and how seriously, this pathway is followed depends entirely on fortuitous circumstances of staff quality, professionalism and opportunity.

The test of any programme, formal or informal, is its effectiveness. If interventions in school are not effective, the *Code of Practice* calls for outside intervention (that is, stage 3 of the code). But outside agencies are often called in at the last minute as a crisis measure, and do not have time to develop a comprehensive approach. Regrettably, when in-school programmes fail, schools often reject the pupil instead of the strategy.

▓▓▓ Pathway 4: 'The final solution'

Sometimes, a sufficiently extreme incident provides the head teacher with grounds to permanently exclude a pupil. In more chronic cases, there is a balance between good and bad behaviour which is sufficiently ambiguous, on paper, to make permanent exclusion difficult to justify. In these cases, the key processes leading to permanent exclusion are informal and covert and contravene equal-opportunities policy and any reasonable service standards. This social (as opposed to the formal) exclusion of the pupil hurts the pupil and their family most of all, because pupils are often unable to help themselves. The sad little cliché that 'it's a cry for help' is, sadly, true. This unhealthy and unacknowledged process is the antithesis of the *Code of Practice*. It, too, has five stages:

1. fragmentation of staff;

2. pressure on senior managers;

3. collusion;

4. scapegoating;

5. aftermath.

Fragmentation of staff

Some staff – often newly qualified and less confident individuals, but sometimes more experienced staff for whom control and authority are key issues – are drawn into the role of 'victim'. (For more on victim teachers, read Stewart and Joines, 1991). Unable to find strategies for managing the pupil's behaviour, they are left feeling undermined and demeaned. They return to the staff room emotionally drained and angry. Because the deskilling experience of failure in the class carries a guilty overtone, resulting feelings of inadequacy cannot be publicly expressed and addressed. Other staff, who are in the role of 'rescuer' to the pupil's 'victim', have much more positive experiences based probably around a facility for finding effective in-class strategies.

However, one expectation of teamwork is mutual support, and so a sympathetic response is required from others to the emotional discharge of the victim teacher's complaint. Attempts to offer suggestions for alternative strategies will reinforce feelings of failure, and may not be be well received, in an informal setting. This staffroom scenario in which one teacher sounds off, others concur, and others keep silent because it is not expedient to disagree, if repeated often enough, provides the material for a colloquial consensus: so-and-so is 'a pain in the neck', a 'troublemaker', 'a disruptive influence' and finally 'on their way out!'.

Pressure on senior managers

Once this consensus forms, even in formal settings such as team meetings moderate teachers find an alternative view hard to promote, because of the risk that the unacknowledged but implicitly recognised feelings could lead to outbursts, accusations and hostility. Senior managers will sometimes try to reduce the tendency of staff teams to fragment into cliques by supporting the consensus and stifling discussion. After all, 'staff must continue to work together'. The expectation is that 'something will be done', and senior managers have only the options already described; the inadequacies of institutional responses to human problems become very apparent.

The SENCoP route is long term and will not be seen as addressing the immediate problems. Real efforts to address the problem depend largely on the commitment and abilities of individual staff members. Application of the behaviour management policy with increasing firmness will meet with approval because it contains that element of retribution for which the injured feelings of the victim teachers cry out. When the genuine efforts (which are informal and therefore unregulated) of the committed staff fail, the clamour increases for further action. If appropriate strategies are hard to find, application of the behaviour management policy – if it is comprehensively formulated – will always provide the illusion of positive action. However, this policy (although according to behavioural theory it should reduce unacceptable behaviour) is in practice mainly retributive and punitive. Hence it does not produce the required change. Improved behaviour following punishment is usually a cognitive response, often mediated by parents, which simply mimics behavioural theory.

Collusion

The staff must now move from consensus to collusion, and implicitly work towards a position of strength. The noticeboard will blandly note that the relevant senior manager 'would like all staff to record any incidents involving the target pupil and pass these to the senior manager's office, so that progress can be monitored'. The oral message passed around the staff room is to 'write down *EVERYTHING* he does!'. Even if the 'rescuer' teachers do not respond enthusiastically, the victimised teachers more than make up for this. Positive reports, if any are made, may be ignored – they don't fit. There is an advocate for the prosecution (the senior manager) but not for the defence!

Scapegoating

The catharsis of feelings of victimisation requires a scapegoat, because such feelings cannot be owned by the victim teacher. If they could, the outcome of bad lessons would have been dialogue, reappraisal, and a new approach (which is just what the 'rescuer' teachers have achieved). It is certainly the case that excluded children are punished for the transgressions of their peers. After all, this is true for all pupils at some point in their education. The consequences are simply much more serious for the excludee because of the context.

The disciplinary procedures in schools are generally without jurisprudence, and charging, sentencing and conviction would be judged unsafe by normal legal standards. For instance, in one London school a pupil was permanently excluded for allegedly threatening another pupil with a small empty plastic bottle (staff did not witness this). The permanent exclusion occurred unexpectedly at a meeting with the head teacher when the pupil's mother lost her temper. In the same school a week later, and possibly as part of a guilty reaction, the same head decided not to exclude a pupil who had actually kicked a member of staff!

A file of more or less prejudicial reports is compiled. Incidents are inflated, and written reports often make an incident sound more serious than the events might justify, through the use of inflationary language ('assault on a female member of staff' to describe an arm petulantly flung out). These reports are judged by the prosecution, and conviction and sentencing is carried out by the same body. Once the file is ready, 'victim' staff wait with anticipation for the one incident needed to trigger the rejection of the pupil. Permanent exclusion can follow a relatively minor event, and parents who promptly challenge the head teacher are often shocked to read the thick file of incident reports, and copies of the letters sent to them – which they had treated as just another message that their child had been in trouble again, a mere formality, although to a professional eye they clearly carried the coded warnings.

The effect of this covert process on the behaviour of pupils is potentially damaging. Pupils are watched more vigilantly, and every misdemeanour is now noted, so that their behaviour may seem to have deteriorated. Their confidence will be further undermined by more or less indirect remarks (pupils often report that they were told, in no uncertain terms, *'We don't want you at this school'*). Attempts by other teachers or the pupils themselves to improve matters may be pre-empted or sabotaged; for instance, subject teachers have been known to refuse to teach a pupil, sometimes leaving them outside the class, unsupervised and liable to incur the disapproval of passing teachers or get involved in corridor incidents.

At the extreme end of the scale, pupils are occasionally subjected to obvious entrapment, and frequently take the blame on the grounds that 'it usually is them, anyway'. One subtle approach used is the 'give them enough rope' technique. Children who are destined for permanent exclusion often find themselves suddenly free of all sanctions or control. They wander around the school, skip lessons, do no work and are not punished for misdemeanours but simply sent out to 'find the head', 'go to the quiet room', etc. Each event results, however, in a written referral. The pupil is enjoying a brief stay in a phoney paradise, a limbo. Pupils who need clear boundaries, a firm disciplinary structure and raised (not lowered) expectations become increasingly unfit for schooling and detached from the educative process. The written referrals and the pupil's increasingly erratic behaviour reliably lead to a departure from the school – one way or the other.

Permanent exclusion is increasingly likely unless the informal efforts of the senior teachers predominate. Usually fixed-term exclusions precede permanent exclusions. Some pupils will choose to modify their behaviour in order to avoid this, and in doing so surprise their critics. However, as Imich (1994) found, there is little evidence that fixed-term exclusions lead to improvement in pupil behaviour. Formal efforts, either as part of the SEN process or any learning or behaviour support initiatives to address the problem, are fine if they work. If they do not the lack of flexibility in the system and the limitations of school resources may hamper effective action. This is, in part, a reflection of the high numbers of pupils who present behaviour problems in secondary school. The overload in the system may encourage the use of covert strategies as the only way to 'get something done'.

Aftermath

Following permanent exclusion a new status quo forms. Teachers are relieved, temporarily, of a problem. However, a new 'public enemy number one' will appear on the scene. The dynamic of a classroom requires that key roles are filled, and one of these seems to be the role of 'antagonist to the teacher'. Besides, disturbance and disruption are a fact of classroom life and are relative to the ambient equilibrium.

Beyond the question of why a pupil has been excluded lies the question of what path the pupil now wishes to follow, which is heavily affected by feelings, anxieties and expectations around the possibility of a return to school.

The 'victim' teacher's view is that the pupil deserved the exclusion. Justifications are mainly two in number:

- *'It was done for the good of the other pupils'* (a statement that may contain some elements of truth).

- *'Now the authority will have to provide the special care needed'* (a statement so loaded as to admit no further discussion here).

The 'rescuer' teacher's view is that effective action other than exclusion could and should have been taken 'for everyone's benefit'. However, the school failed to find effective strategies to achieve this and the 'rescuer' teacher will not enhance his or her position in the school by voicing views which implicitly criticise both the victims and the senior management up to the head teacher and governors. There is always likely to be a group of pupils (however small this group might become as schools become better skilled and resourced in an ideal world) whose needs go beyond what even the best of staff can provide.

However, there is a cohort of excludees (even under the present system) whose behaviour, in another school, might have been accommodated and modified without the need for exclusion. There is also a cohort of excludees whose needs could have been met by the school, supported by the kind of approach being advocated here – effective action is possible, but a change of culture may be needed to achieve it.

Although an appeals process exists, many parents and pupils take the reasonable view that to seek to return to a school which has so emphatically rejected them is by varying degrees humiliating, counterproductive and generally self-defeating. Alternatively the process may simply be too difficult for some parents to manage. The pupil will feel a powerful sense of failure, and an immediate loss of a significant factor affecting identity. Feelings of anger, injustice, premature loss and uncertainty will manifest. There may be over-reaction, and strongly felt assertions of antisocial intent which can be very unproductive. Underlying all this, the deep sense of failure will demand a personal reappraisal of the future. Many parents of excluded children were themselves excludees or children with special needs. Their own children's experiences reinforce their view of schools as rejecting and condemning institutions, and parents and children reinforce one another's feeling and experience, creating a double stumbling block for both.

Parents, nevertheless, are now required (under crisis conditions) to become experts without training, in order to identify possible schools and obtain interviews. The parents' agenda is to find the best school possible, and at first well-known sink schools which frequently have surplus places are rejected. Later there may be some dismay when the pupil is forced to apply there, or the pupil may refuse to attend at all. The school's agenda is generally to keep excluded pupils out if possible. The staff consensus is that additional problems are not their concern.

The schools with enviable reputations are generally full. Schools with vacant places may employ a variety of techniques to avoid accepting unwanted pupils. One of these is to invoke the 'waiting list'.

Pupils come on and go off roll throughout the school year, and the common perception that schools have stable populations is false, particularly in inner cities. Commonly, parents seeking a school place (for reasons other than exclusion) will apply to a number of schools, and these names are added to the waiting list unless a place is immediately available, or the school is waiting for the parent to make a decision. Such lists rapidly become corrupt, and many of the pupils on it have already found an alternative place. Nevertheless, the parent of an excluded pupil will be put off by the knowledge that their child is at the end of a list and will probably not check back on a regular basis.

A second approach adopted by some schools is to refuse to accept a pupil on inadequate grounds, and rely on ignorance of the legal position or parental inadequacy to protect them. One school refused entry to a Year 10 pupil because there were no places in Year 9! Once refused, the only option is an appeal, with all the difficulties and delays this entails. Schools naturally operate on a broad time-scale and it is not unknown to wait five or six months from the date of first application before the formal hearing. Authorities who should oversee the process may be reluctant to be drawn into a battle of wills and lay down the law over one particular pupil, especially one who has been excluded.

These experiences reinforce the feelings of rejection experienced by pupil and parent. Months pass, holidays intervene and the options narrow. Carl Parsons (1995) found that only 15–20 per cent of secondary pupils returned to mainstream school.

▨ Tackling the exclusion culture

Earlier in this chapter some suggestions were made for encouraging an inclusive ethos. The substance of those suggestions will find fertile ground amongst the many teachers who can readily appreciate the humanity of their pupils and, indeed, their own fallibility. The promotion of those suggestions provides the context for individual work with specific teachers around specific pupils. However, individual teachers also need special support to achieve their educational targets.

Michael's case study earlier in this chapter (p. 61) provides a good example of the way the exclusion process can be deflected. The important point was that the dynamic of exclusion was achieved through good communication, not by telling staff they were doing things wrongly. Some staff were mishandling the 'Michael situation'(p. 61) because they lacked the information needed to make better decisions. *Once staff were given the relevant information they adopted alternative approaches which reduced the need to exclude Michael. However, other teachers, who did not have any special information, were already able to accommodate his needs. Clearly, some staff do have sufficient empathy and social skills to cope with difficult children.*

It should not come as a shock to senior managers to hear that some staff are more skilled than others. However, the logic of this situation is that pupils are being excluded because some teachers cannot manage them. An extremely pragmatic approach is needed here. A similar argument might apply, for instance, to pupils' exam scores. Those who had better teachers do better as a group and as individuals. It is obviously the aim of every head teacher to improve the quality of staff in the school both collectively and individually. In seeking to reduce exclusion, long-term (management by design) initiatives and short-term (crisis management) interventions are needed. The remainder of this section looks at longer term measures for helping individual staff to cope better.

Provide professional development

Staff will improve their skills more quickly with help. Creative management is needed here. Whole-school INSET days are only one opportunity. Staff probably learn most quickly through coaching and 'self-help groups', in which many good ideas, tricks of the trade and imaginative techniques increase their repertoire of skills. General insight and understanding will develop best under neutral conditions such as twilight sessions and the occasional 'outing with training'. Remember, the skills being developed are not just helping the problem child, but also the many children who are difficult sometimes, those who are going to be at risk of failure later on, and indirectly all the children, who will be working in a less confrontational atmosphere.

Don't get stuck with one 'big idea' for behaviour management (though there should be a unified behaviour policy). One solution is unlikely to work for everyone. Teachers need to own the techniques they use, so having a mix of different approaches not only increases the skills base, it also increases the likelihood that every teacher will find at least one way to tackle problems – developing a sense of autonomy and empowerment amongst the staff.

Train senior staff to facilitate

'Training the trainers' courses can be hugely effective in extending training skills, and hence the opportunities for professional development amongst junior staff via senior staff. It is a much more flexible and economic way of providing targeted training. Facilitation skills such as active listening and group working will enable senior managers to facilitate all staff meetings better, as well as parent meetings, sharing good-practice sessions, and informal professional development opportunities. In particular, every member of staff should have a mentor to whom they can talk confidentially if the need arises.

Encourage 'fallible' culture

Staff should be encouraged to recognise and admit their mistakes – everyone makes mistakes, including the head teacher and other staff with seniority and experience. In one school, the head kept a book outside his office in which pupils could write down any complaints they had about staff. All complaints made were investigated. It was a way of making pupils feel listened to, and reminding staff that their practice was not above criticism by their 'clients'. Naturally, many of the complaints were proved groundless and this too formed part of the learning process.

Help staff to keep things in proportion

Pupil's misdemeanours are often trifling in the wider context. A culture of self-deprecation and wry humour will help staff to release some of the built-up tensions safely. School life, like games, should generally not be taken too seriously.

Encourage staff to rise to the challenge

Disruptive behaviour is sometimes called 'challenging behaviour'. This is a valuable reconstruction of the context. It is part of the school culture and hence part of the job. It may be irritating, but 'final solutions' involving the complete rejection of a child are in most cases worse than the offences that prompted them. (For instance, only about 12 permanent exclusions in each 1000 are a result of assaults on staff.)

Establish a culture of non-exclusion, with senior management team back-up

Downward pressure on exclusion rates can be achieved by reducing expectations amongst staff that exclusion is high on the 'options for sanctions' list. There is very strong evidence that the harder it is to exclude the less often it happens. In particular, avoid automatic exclusions for particular behaviours.

Monitor and publish data showing how individual teachers rate on 'behaviour' scores

This will ensure that positive referrals are as highly valued as negative ones. Other publishable data include: number of referrals to the withdrawal room, number of parent liaison meetings held, number of detentions given, and so on. The main thing is to highlight the positives.

Establish no-blame sharing of responsibility

Staff will feel threatened by any management decisions or initiatives which appear to shift blame on to their shoulders. This is completely understandable, and right. Blame does not really enter the equation – only responsibility. One can make the analogy that the doctor does not make us ill, but has a responsibility to make us better. The less defensive staff feel, the more they will be able to accommodate in their thinking the idea that the issues are primarily about relationships, and that they are part of those. It is *not* a matter of blame, and skilful PR will ensure that staff get the right message.

Initiate a policy of 'delayed decision-making'

The temptation to act quickly to deal with incidents should usually (though not always) be avoided. For minor incidents it matters less. When the events are likely to culminate in a serious sanction like exclusion it is important to give everyone time to reflect, and individual teachers concerned should have a chance to reconsider their assessment of events. This will only really work if the other strategies suggested here are in place. Staff should have a chance to say: 'I could have done things differently', and feel able to negotiate with the pupil over their behaviour in future.

Develop a prevention culture

Pessimists frequently use the 'resources' argument against proponents of progressive approaches. They argue that these kinds of solution are too time-consuming and indeed take resources away from 'more deserving cases'. This is a specious and politically motivated argument. Taking the time early on in the development of a difficult behaviour syndrome to deal with the problems thoroughly and effectively will save masses of time later on. Secondly, many of the measures proposed in this chapter are substitutive. That is, they replace other approaches which carry the same, or indeed a higher, time cost.

The strategies suggested in the next chapter may be more likely to require additional resourcing, but the government is currently committed to putting those extra resources in place. Nothing less than a cultural shift is under way now, and over time resources will move from the hugely expensive 'special sector' into schools for just this purpose. Part of this movement is the need to shift from sanctions to prevention.

Crisis management

A crucial element in the process described above (pathways to exclusion) is the pressure put on senior managers to 'do something'. Senior managers have to take responsibility for exclusion and are often pivotal in deciding outcomes. As a general rule of thumb there are two kinds of incident.

First there are those in which there has been a clear breech of the behaviour policy, often admitted to by the pupil(s) concerned and easily explained. Pupils may have drawn graffiti on walls, or got into fights; or another pupil is plaintiff, having been bullied, had property damaged; and so on. In these cases the issue is probably one in which the teacher is little more than a reporter after the fact.

Then there are those cases where the 'plaintiff' is the teacher and the situation has a confrontational dimension. Perhaps a pupil has not been behaving satisfactorily and has refused to carry out tasks as required. Here the attitude of the teacher is as important as the attitude of the pupil. Is the teacher angry, or upset? Are there indications that stress levels are much too high? A stressed or angry teacher cannot communicate positively with a stressed pupil. What evidence is there that imaginative attempts were made to deflect the problem? If the incident fits a pattern of confrontation and disruption, what efforts were made prior to the incident to ensure that the pattern was not repeated? If the teacher has pastoral responsibility, what efforts have been made to liaise with home, to involve peers (if appropriate) or to spend some time on a one-to-one basis?

This analysis relies on the idea that the teacher is not to blame for the problem, but *is* responsible for finding a solution. Teachers will be more successful with difficult pupils if they take the approach that the pupil is not to blame either, but *is* responsible for his or her own behaviour. The only culprit is the culture in which we live and which we are mutually trying to change for the better.

Senior staff should give teachers who are handing in negative referrals some quality time themselves – a chance to sit and talk about the problem child and unburden themselves. This is where listening skills come into play. If teachers are counselled in the right way, issues may well arise which prove to have little to do with the individual pupil who was presenting as the problem.

Senior staff should also empathise with the teacher over the problem and give assurances of moral support in the difficulties, offering active support through advice and guidance, ideally demonstrating by example how to deal with the situation better.

Consideration should be given to setting up a meeting between the teacher and the pupil, and using mediation and negotiation skills (demonstrating by example the empathic no-blame approach) to support both sides towards a reconciliation.

■ Step-by-step guide

How does a school begin to set up an inclusive infrastructure? What are the school management issues to be considered?

Firstly, it is a broad-based approach that is required, rather than a single initiative. For young people in their formative years, every experience is developmental, and may set in train a sequence of defining events. It calls to mind the children's nursery rhyme which ends 'For want of a king the country was lost, and all for the want of a nail.' For instance, on a bad day, acting on bad advice, a head teacher excludes a pupil for three days. Mum leaves for work early and so it is easy for the pupil to conceal the letter rather than face the music. But the consequence is that no-one is keeping an eye on him and he wanders the streets meeting up with some older boys in the park who persuade him to try a joint. The narcotic effects of this drug reduce his feelings of anxiety and guilt and he is keen to continue to use it. Six months later, the pupil is facing permanent exclusion, mum is in despair, and precious school time and resources have been spent first trying to manage a problem, and then drafting paperwork and setting up meetings to eliminate it. It is not an uncommon story.

On the other hand, whole-school initiatives to reduce truancy and absence and prevent exclusion can work in the opposite way. Or a home visit instead of the exclusion might have illuminated the difficulties at home, and opened up some possibilities for helping the pupil cope better and arrive at school in a more positive frame of mind. There is a great deal any school can do to reduce the number of marginalised children. Most of the strategies in this list do not require any additional expenditure – and remember, reductions in problematic and disruptive events, less management of negative referrals, and a more positive ethos all increase the effectiveness of resources and help to raise all pupils' attainments:

1. Devise a whole-school plan for inclusion which will develop integrated systems incrementally over time.

2. Ensure staff understand that the school is developing an inclusive culture, why this is so, what it all means, and how staff will be supported to achieve it.

3. Consider the management-of-change issues involved in promoting steps 1 and 2. Staff attititudes need to change, and this requires developing staff awareness. A skilfully managed consultation and project development plan will increase the likelihood that staff will feel a sense of ownership of, and commitment to, the project. *Disaffected staff need as much help as disaffected children.*

4. Assess and revise as necessary whole-school policies as they apply to behaviour management and system of rewards so that they are consistent and fairly applied – codes of conduct should be seen as applicable to staff and students alike, and pupils should also have a way of making complaints, mediated by a senior manager.

5. Assess and revise as necessary the communications infrastructure within the school to reduce paperwork as much as possible and ensure effective information sharing.

6. Ensure that all staff have a school mentor who can actively support and advise them.

7. Review training and development needs for staff to increase the skills base, especially with respect to interpersonal relations.

8. Enlist the support of all the pupils, by developing group work, peer mentoring projects, schools councils, and anti-bullying programmes.

9. Constantly review your policy on bullying and ensure that children are able to give feedback in confidence. Target the problem rather than the pupils involved (i.e. try new group anti-bullying initiatives rather than punishing individuals).

10. Tackle truancy by applying the DfEE guidance (1999). The guidance is very strong on this point.

11. Audit, review and develop the SEN department within the school, ensuring SEN staff have administrative support and professional development.

12. Extend the value of this resource to all pupils and staff, by encouraging the SEN Co-ordinator and support staff to share their expertise more widely. Senior managers can set an example to other staff by attending twilight and groupwork sessions themselves.

13. Develop home–school communications and liaison, probably based in the SEN department. This provision is essential for involving parents earlier and following up after reintegration.

14. Develop a parent participation programme – parents are already invited to school events. Explore ways to increase the value to

parents of such events, perhaps by extending their scope. Add in new events, start a parent support group, and enlist volunteer parents to help. Other voluntary agencies such as the local church may provide volunteer support to give this a boost. Ask parents for feedback (questionnaires can be filled when parents come to talk to the class teacher) – what would they like more of? Are there better times to hold events? Monitor non-attendance of parents at school events – this is a bad sign and it might be worth following up.

15. Develop links with other schools, possibly by sharing INSET sessions and disseminating good practice.

16. Develop a protocol for arranging managed moves between schools for at-risk pupils.

17. Plan jointly with other head teachers to devise effective local strategies; then lobby the local education authority to support its development and implementation. It is essential to open up dialogue within education and across the community to ensure that there is concerted action.

18. Build links with voluntary bodies locally, including churches, charities and youth organisations (but first confirm that they police-check all their staff) by inviting them to participate in school events, give presentations or organise one-off group sessions.

19. Build links with other services locally, including the EWS, the EPS, social services, health services and the police. Invite them to talk to staff and share their insights on the problem.

20. Assess the viability of different models for outreach work. This could mean jointly funding outreach workers with other schools, education centres or services. Alternatively, you might buy worker time from a voluntary or statutory agency (but see Chapter 8 on who does what and when).

Start to write a funding application *now*. In the short term the government is set to distribute about £450 million to education for projects to reduce exclusion and truancy. Later there is bound to be pressure for more resources. Ensure that your local education authority is keeping you informed about money that is available. To write an application you need to have set in place as much of the above as possible. *Projects will suggest themselves as you start to implement some of these strategies.*

The crucial thing is to develop outreach work, and this is discussed at length in the next chapter. However, the question of who does this must be decided. If you have reached (or even jumped to) step 20 in the list above then you will be in a position to develop, with others, an integrated approach to outreach work and reintegration. However, it is perfectly possible to start 'growing' your outreach team now, using the school's SEN department and other non-teaching staff. Encourage them to work flexibly on and off site.

This chapter has focused more or less entirely on changing the school side. I think it is right to put that first, and to try to get our house in order. But of course the pupils themselves are the main problem-holders, and the next chapter looks at what can be done to get to the heart of that issue.

5 Developing outreach work from the school base

It has been claimed that two-thirds of disruptive children settle down spontaneously and stop being a problem. Keith Topping (1983) apparently found 'massive evidence' to this effect. However, at the chalk-face, it does not seem like it. It is not difficult to imagine how Mrs Potts from Class 9M would react if, on reporting that Sam had been breathing heavily on Sasha's neck and making obscene suggestions again, she was told by the head-of-year: 'Not to worry, it will probably remit spontaneously!'

Despite the need to support teachers and protect children, most people in the profession would agree that, to varying degrees, everyone loses out when the only course of action seems to be exclusion. A great deal is made of partnership, which is surely one of the enduring of all buzz-words; but school failure is a partnership too. As with animal euthanasia, the basic principle supporting exclusion is expediency.

- Excluded pupils are generally unhappy and full of mistrust, and they are often confused.

- They feel that they are losing control, adding to the anxiety they may be feeling as a result of a wide variety of losses and other negative life-events which have left them with a residue of anger, guilt and depression.

- They are often desperately worried about their academic deficits, which they nevertheless foolishly try to cover up.

- There is frequently a powerful sense of injustice. They have contributed to their predicament, and that contribution stems from the set of dysfunctional attitudes and beliefs, about the world, themselves, teachers and learning, and unhelpful opinions about the way schools should and do operate.

- There are frequently family difficulties involving conflict, stress and abuse.

- They have sometimes become involved with the police, and may have a police record. Social services may also be involved. In fact there is often a long history of failed agency involvement. Sometimes, they are involved with a delinquent peer group, and have a potentially destructive experience of street-life.

- Finally, there is often a lack of awareness on their part of their potential for positive action, and their qualities go unrecognized or undervalued.

A Statement of Needs indicating 'mainstream school with support' could be generated for some, or even all, regularly or permanently excluded pupils. However, the weight of argument is against this. A local education authority would reasonably resist any attempt to increase systematically the numbers of Statements written. The statementing process is a blunt instrument, and where agencies disagreed as to the appropriate provision, this could powerfully mitigate against the flexible, immediate and hands-on approach to reintegration. The statementing process can be long and cumbersome, and would tie up resources. Finally, any successful reintegration project should have as its objective the empowerment of pupils to succeed in school without additional support. Only after considering these points can one say that, in some cases, statementing might contribute to the success of reintegration, particularly at Key Stage 2. In the majority of cases, support at stage 3 of the SENCoP is much more appropriate.

■ Getting someone involved

Schools already have disciplinary systems in place, and senior managers, subject teachers and class tutors should understand their pastoral responsibilities. When a pupil is showing signs of chronic or substantial behaviour problems and tutors are obliged to offer sanctions, this could be viewed as a *de facto* stage 1 SENCoP intervention, although pupils are not going to be formally placed on the SEN register for everyday misdemeanours.

At this stage, parents should be involved, and encouraged to help their child to understand and remain within the school's behaviour management system. If the problem is persistent and has not been improved by this level of involvement over a period of time, opposition to the pupil will increase and senior managers will be drawn into the process of trying to do something systematic. The school can take a more thorough look at this level and how the problems are arising. Some of the solid and sensible suggestions made elsewhere in this book, and through guidance issued by the DfEE and other organisations, may well sort out the problem. There are practical difficulties in ensuring that intervention at an early stage happens for children who turn out to need it:

- In most schools, there are many frequent minor events which involve some sort of sanction.

- There may even be quite a number of pupils who are effectively at 'stage 2', inasmuch as senior managers are involved in planning remedial action.

- Carefully appraising these pupils on an on-going basis may not be a realistic option.

- Incidents frequently involve groups of pupils and it may not be practicable to treat one differently from the others.

- Some pupils have only one or two short exclusions, before modifying their behaviour and moving back into broadly acceptable behaviour patterns.

For all these reasons, it is difficult for schools to know who and when to refer to outside agencies ('stage 3'). Once it becomes clear that this is necessary, considerable antagonism may have already built up on both sides. It is therefore preferable to involve outside agencies earlier, but in practice there is the danger that their effectiveness may be compromised by the high number of superfluous cases.

The pupil might be referred to an outreach worker from one of the recognised agencies such as educational welfare, or social services. There are also a growing number of voluntary agencies and organisations that could provide outreach workers. Schools might also develop their own service either alone, or with a consortium of schools. There are numerous possibilities for collaboration, which rely on the creativity and determination of senior managers for their implementation. The spin-offs are also numerous – a school that can reduce exclusion rates is likely to be serving the pastoral needs of all its pupils better.

It will be clear from what follows that the social psychology of the relationships between pupil, family and school are considered very important.

There is absolutely no reason why any member of the school staff cannot carry out the reintegration work which marginalised pupils need. However, roles and functions cannot be mixed up in a haphazard way. Heads-of-year cannot be handing out sanctions one minute and expecting the pupil to come into their office and disclose sensitive information the next!

There are ways around this – changing settings from in-school to out-of-school may help, for example. Professionals can try to show they have another side to their character, especially by demonstrating a different style, accompanied by clear behavioural distinctions such as agreeing, for the purposes of the process, to first names and by modelling disclosure behaviour by talking about themselves as non-professionals. Many professionals would find this very hard, which is a good measure of how hard it is for pupils to do this. Here is one of many challenges presented by this work.

■ The outreach worker

In this context, 'outreach worker' means the person who has been given responsibility for steering the course of the intervention. It could be a member of teaching staff, a specialist worker employed by the school, or someone brought in from an outside agency. *It is important to restrict the number of outreach workers involved over time as much as possible, avoiding professional overload for the family in particular who will rapidly grow confused if too many professionals end up on the doorstep.*

Clearly, the outreach worker will play a decisive role in the success or failure of reintegration. Within community services one often seems to find two types of professional. *Experience-based professionals*:

■ are practitioner's with limited qualifications and training;

■ are already working within communities close to the 'front-line';

■ relate well to young people;

■ easily understand or adopt an inside perspective;

■ may already be using a hands-on approach;

■ are less happy with the technical aspects of assessment and intervention;

■ find it more difficult to build structure;

■ lack confidence in liaising at a strategic level with the senior management team;

■ have less authority.

In contrast, *postgraduate professionals*:

■ are highly trained;

■ are well-qualified;

- have extensive skills and understanding;

- could be a powerful force for change;

- are competent at the appropriate level;

- are trained to preserve professional autocracy;

- lack hands-on experience;

- feel uncomfortable about applying skills outside the 'professional culture';

- are alienated from the client group by social class and/or culture;

- are professionally disempowered by institutional culture.

Outreach workers could come from either group. The former need training, and the latter need to be empowered to take their skills back into the community. Some believe it is unprofessional to provide their services outside the clinic or centre, and some are reluctant for personal reasons to do so.

Both the experience-based and the postgraduate professional need to be set free from excessive paperwork, because the former group find it hard to do and the latter group tend to use it as a substitute for real client engagement. The function of paperwork is, in any case, frequently illusory. It makes staff feel they are being monitored and supervised (or scrutinised and mistrusted), and it provides evidence of management for when the auditors and inspectors call. Yes, there can be records and reports, but their production is too often a tedious and ineffective task. It is well known that people filling in pro-formas feel anxious unless most of each box is filled with writing. Managers can make their staff more efficient at a stroke simply by making all the boxes on their report forms smaller.

In one London education programme an overzealous support teacher made a suggestion, which was accepted, that there should be a report on each pupil session, and an A4 pro-forma was duly drafted. But simple arithmetic showed that, with 15 pupils each having 12 sessions per week, over 2000 pages of text would be generated each term – a pile of paper nearly ten inches high. Who was going to read the reports, and why? In another service, support teachers have to provide reports on each pupil each term. All very well perhaps, but in order to make sure each one sounds 'professional' the service manager has handed out a sheet with standardised sample phrases. (This is not a new idea – the same approach has been advocated for filling in, amongst other things, profiles for National Records of Achievement.) Surely something has been lost here!

Just as there are two kinds of professional, there are two kinds of knowledge-base:

■ On the one hand there is good practice which is unevaluated, unrecorded and undisseminated.

■ On the other hand there is a huge body of research findings and innovative programme design which is seen only by other researchers and academics.

It has been said that it takes 20 years for research findings to filter down to the front-line teacher. Somehow, 'crossover' must be achieved. This will happen only when professional barriers are reduced and communications between institutions and cultures are improved. Front-line and community based workers must be less defensive, and more open to learning. Researchers and academics must find a way into the community so that they can share their ideas directly.

Outreach workers should be prepared to commit to their work in a way which is, perhaps, unprecedented. No qualification, professional wisdom or administrative output can substitute for the amount of effort and determination which goes into building the bridge of trust and collaboration between outreach worker, pupil and family – for instance, in the case of Aleem the amount of time spent with the mother trying to get a speech therapist, or being called up at 3am by Hamed's distraught mother trying to get her son out of police custody, or the hours spent sitting in a filthy flat talking to a despairing parent. This isn't heroism, it is part of the social psychology of individual regeneration, and it does have boundaries.

Staff working with children at risk of failure in school need to have the ability to:

■ relate well to people of all ages, genders, and backgrounds
■ understand (without colluding in) the difficulties of parents
■ support adults without creating dependencies
■ interpret behaviour and provide meaning
■ listen to and understand the family's imperatives
■ advocate on behalf of all parties without alienating anyone

within the context of a clear and specific action plan

Figure 9

The Audit Commission (1996) suggests that people delivering remedial programmes need to be specially trained, and selected on the basis of interpersonal skills such as communication skills, warmth, openness, and the ability to set appropriate limits. The commission proposes training in theories of criminal behaviour (i.e. childhood development and learning theory), and several months of specific and general behavioural interventions.

The outreach worker needs to have listening skills, maturity, and a knowledge of different approaches to working with children and families, backed up with a broad understanding (preferably in practice) of the cultures in which education, social, health and local authority procedures operate.

Reintegration work is challenging, innovative, community-based and down-to-earth. It is unique to itself, and the best way (and probably the only way) to become good at it is to do it.

▨ Matching skills to needs

It is clear from what has already been said that professionals will be expected to work across professional boundaries. First, this needs to be justified, and then it needs to be managed safely.

Outreach workers can operate on four levels:

- The outreach worker does everything – liaises, manages, plans, assesses, implements interventions, and evaluates outcomes (with or without support teachers and workers).

- The outreach worker does nearly everything, but accesses other services as necessary in support of the plan, to obtain advice or specific expertise.

- The outreach worker teamworks, managing the whole process but devolving significant parts of its implementation to other professionals who share in planning and evaluation as well.

- With interagency work, the outreach worker is part of a broader operation managed elsewhere and with limited control over the process.

There are a number of reasons why professionals often need to work as multiskilled individuals. Pupils' problems are rectifiable but multiple – the success of this work requires the implementation of a strategy for each problem. But the problems do not limit themselves to single domains, and they are often relatively small. When one community worker recently referred a single mother who had an alcohol problem to the local social services, they were not even prepared to open a duty worker file. He was told:

Is that all? We have mothers on that estate who are heroin addicts and into prostitution. Your case is just not serious enough.

It is simply not practicable to have three or four agencies all involved with one family at the same time. The families do not like it, because it is time-consuming and stressful. Professionals seem to assume that families are just sitting around all day waiting to talk to them. Young mothers with several children may be on the go all day, and have surprisingly busy schedules. If they work, life can be impossibly demanding without the need for meetings and phone calls, and professional appointments can often mean taking a day's leave. The effectiveness of each agency can be undermined by the need for clients to go over the same ground again and again, disclosing less each time and probably becoming more cynical. Pupils and parents can become confused about who is in charge, and get mixed messages.

The effectiveness of outreach work is greatly enhanced if the outreach worker is able to act quickly and independently. Communications are simpler, and professional know-how and networking skills mean that, where services and resources are needed, the outreach worker can access them more easily, and often more cheaply. If the outreach worker does not do it, no-one else will – there is no-one else available to tackle the small but important array of problems which underlie a particular pupil's problems. One solution is to encourage the development of what has been called 'barefoot working'. The 'barefoot doctors' were paramedical workers who were operating in Africa from the nineteenth century. There has always been a shortage of medical personnel and resources in the more remote but inhabited parts of Africa. Consequently, partly trained paramedics were given permission to practise medicine as best they could, using whatever materials they could.

■ Teamworking

Figure 10 distinguishes between two kinds of joint working practice. The idea of teamwork is that groups of professionals should get together and pool their resources, experience and energies. It is a wonderful idea in theory, and it can work. However, unless teamwork is built into the infrastructure, there is always the danger that teamworking becomes team-failing. Professionals may fall out on personal terms with other team members; have very different levels of expertise, confidence and authority; not understand each other's working cultures; or not share each other's objectives. Most importantly, communications may take up too much of their time.

```
┌─────────────────────────────────────────────────────────┐
│  ┌──────────────────────────────────────────────────┐   │
│  │                                                    │   │
│  │  Teamwork working                                  │   │
│  │  Professionals agree on:                           │   │
│  │  ■  one line manager                               │   │
│  │  ■  one plan                                       │   │
│  │  ■  one culture                                    │   │
│  │  ■  interdependence                                │   │
│  │  ■  ease of communication                          │   │
│  │                                                    │   │
│  │  Teamwork failing                                  │   │
│  │  = Fragmented management                           │   │
│  │  ■  different planning and procedural systems      │   │
│  │  ■  alien cultures                                 │   │
│  │  ■  success criteria different                     │   │
│  │  ■  communication is always a problem              │   │
│  │                                                    │   │
│  └──────────────────────────────────────────────────┘   │
└─────────────────────────────────────────────────────────┘
```

Figure 10

There are three ways to build teamwork into the infrastructure:

■ *Develop and empower professionals to act with a high degree of autonomy to collaborate with other professionals on an* ad hoc *basis.* This approach is the most flexible and easily adapted but it may be liable to attrition from managers who want to claw back their workers to perform their core functions. The 'development with empowerment' approach does require a high level of competence and commitment from professionals involved, and its failings – though no greater than with the other two approaches – may be more apparent. Nevertheless, this approach may be ideal for local initiatives, such as a consortium of schools.

■ *Set up multidisciplinary teams with clear mandates and line management.* These teams should not fragment because each professional is answerable to the same manager, whose job it is to provide coherence. Such teams can be small and flexible in approach, sharing cases or assigning them to individual workers on the basis of need. Nevertheless there are some extra costs in establishing and maintaining such teams, and once established they cannot be disbanded easily, and may be at times underutilised or overstretched.

■ *Adopt the case conference approach.* In a way this is an amalgam of the other two approaches, since case conferences are case-specific and at the same time formally make arrangements to share involvement in a case. Case conferences are not immune from 'team failure'.

Their chief characteristic is momentum (which may be either uphill or downhill). They can take a long time to set up, planning developments can be difficult to implement, and they take up a huge amount of human resources. When there is a high level of agreement around the table, a great deal can get done. They are the main instrument for formally involving social services in educational cases. Case conferences are, in practice, limited to the most serious cases and this is just as well.

Some strategic planning is needed to work out how agencies can operate together. There is a danger that discussions may drift into the devising of a new set of procedural guidelines which create more work for practitioners without bringing the goal of real partnership any closer. Forums for interagency discussion should try to include representatives of parents and ethnic minorities so that their views can be heard.

At the end of the day, outreach workers are likely to be doing most of the work themselves, most of the time. They need support, encouragement, guidance and resources from line managers to do so. How can line managers be sure that outreach workers are not stepping outside their boundary of competence?

Figure 11 shows in graphic form the kind of assessment outreach workers need to do personally before proceeding. They should first make their own assessment of their skills or technical knowledge, competence and confidence in various spheres of activity (the larger ovals in the diagram show higher levels of overall expertise). They should then make an assessment of the needs of the pupil. This estimation may reflect the particular make-up of the family or other situational factors. Each spike in the diagram represents one issue requiring action, the lengths of the spikes reflecting the severity of the problems.

In the example given, the professional would probably decide that the level of concern over child-protection issues did not warrant a referral to social services, and that other issues around family life fell within the professional's competence. The academic deficits are such that a specialist assessment of specific learning difficulties could be valuable, although this is borderline, and would have to be considered in the light of the overall cost of the pupils' programme.

However, the very serious problems created by the pupil's anger and frustration are stretching the professional's skills and creating a crisis of confidence. Specialist advice should be sought, possibly leading to referral to another agency for help in this specific area; but preferably this would be accessed through co-working with colleagues, extending and developing the professional's competence-base in the process.

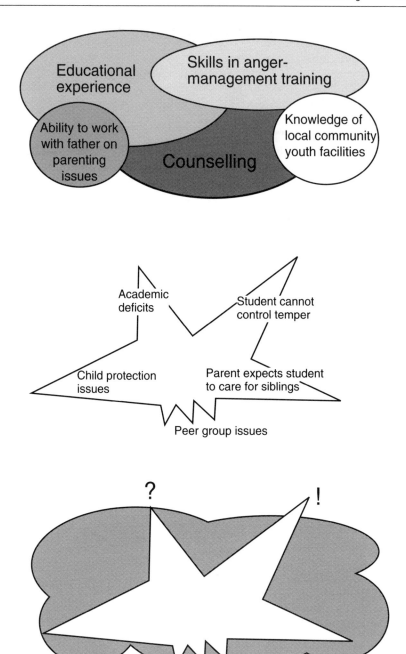

Figure 11

▬ Conflicting time frames

Only the bloody-minded determination of senior managers can counter the 'process conflicts' inherent in this work. Elsewhere, the difficulties involved in identifying those who need this kind of specialist input were discussed. In practice, outside intervention (SENCoP stage 3) for pupils at risk of school failure is likely to come only when alarm bells have been ringing in some quarters for quite some time. The covert rejectionist agendas of stressed and deskilled teachers will be well established and the 'one-last-chance' lobby will be in full cry, safe in the knowledge that the 'one more incident' is inevitable, as a self-fulfilling prophesy. Unfortunately, intervention takes time and an incident can happen without notice.

Humans are rather like plants: some grow faster than others, just as some are hardier than others. However, although very young humans may grow like bamboo, school-aged children, particularly of the adolescent variety, develop slowly – especially when the soil in which they are planted is not very rich in nutrients. Figure 12 shows notional time-frames for various possible aspects of a failing pupil's programme. The time-scale for change contrasts starkly with the repeated opportunities for incidents which the school day affords.

Conflicting time-frames

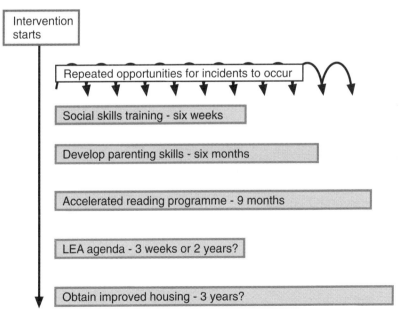

Figure 12

For this reason only, exclusion might be used as way of throwing a *cordon sanitaire* around a pupil, whilst the processes of intervention and change go on. *In the absence of that intervention, exclusion alone is likely to achieve nothing.*

Now that schools can exclude a pupil for up to 45 days in any one school year, it would be possible to give a pupil a really long break from school. However, there are also dangers with such an approach, and it would need to be part of a structured and meaningful way of approaching the pupil's needs, rather than a knee-jerk reaction intended as punishment.

Exclusion should never be used as punishment. It is too harsh. It might be needed as treatment, in the same way that infectious children are quarantined.

In other cases, the senior managers will need to reassure teachers that there is something going on, using the communication strategies shown in Figure 8 on p. 66. Staff who become involved in supporting change in school are more likely to have a positive view of the pupil.

▮ Entering into the real-life drama of the child

Working with children at risk of school failure needs to be understood from a dual perspective. On the one hand there is the intervention process, but on the other there is its dramatization. In many good plays, the author creates some characters whose behaviour and dialogue seem mainly to have a direct effect on the actions of others – for instance, the character of Hamlet, or indeed of the butler Jeeves who appears to understand Bertie Wooster's actions much better than he does himself. The writer has made these characters to seem 'in control', or 'in the know'. The audience's pleasure is enhanced by identifying with this 'author of the actions of others'. Whilst in real life no-one can predict with certainty the outcome of their actions on future events, outreach workers working with excluded children need to conduct the process in such a way that, wherever possible, the pupil and his family feel themselves impelled as if through a good script, to respond in just such a way as the outreach worker would wish, leading to the inevitable and successful result. How can this apparent *tour de force* be accomplished?

The answer is not 'charisma' – this style of working, or *modus operandi*, can be understood as a series of techniques. It may be that the accumulation of life experiences will make the task easier, and there is certainly a moral authority and level of understanding which may come with age, and a personal knowledge of family life and children. But a knowledge of schools and the education system is also a requirement. The outreach worker may acquire the necessary skills by chance or through selection and training.

The earlier dramatic metaphor is a reminder that the world of the young is full of dramas (usually comic tragedies) and that children are likely to respond to appearances far more than adults. The style of the adults around them is therefore no less important to the child than their knowledge of education is to the school. The excluded pupil must grow to like and respect these adults and so must the family, and part of the job is winning people over who may not like or trust teachers, policemen or social workers, or authority figures of any kind.

At this early stage the characterisations of the 'players' (returning to the dramatic metaphor) are most crucial. As a pupil advocate I often introduce myself as follows:

> *You may be wondering who I am. Well, I'm not a teacher; I'm not a social worker; I'm not a therapist; I'm not a policeman; I'm not a youth worker. I'm not here because you're sick; I'm not here because you're bad; I'm not here because you aren't in school. I am here to get you back into school. That's my job. Do you want to go back to school?*

The answer is invariably 'yes', but only time will tell what conditions are attached to that 'yes'. Finding out what is really motivating the pupil is part of the process of comprehensive assessment which precedes intervention. That assessment must explore academic achievement and social functioning in school, domestic circumstances and the parenting infrastructure, and the personality, mental health and social behaviour of the pupil as an individual. Approaches used can vary so long as the outcome is a multidimensional profile which provides the outreach worker with a firm platform from which to launch the second stage in the process.

▨ Style with technique

Frequently success lies in the application of a familiar, and correct, technique but in a new (community) setting. Of course, it isn't the physical locality that is important but the social context which is different. Outreach workers need to understand that: '*You have to join people before you can move them*' (Wolfelt, 1991).

In other words, a bond based on mutual commitment, understanding and (within appropriate boundaries) affection must be given time to form, before the professional can hope to influence people and induce change. Some people are discomforted by words like 'healing' and 'empathy', and if so, the role of outreach worker is probably not for them. There is not always time to get permission before innovations are tried, and the veneer of professionalism needs to be replaced with a non-professional, hands-on, slightly anti-establishment complexion.

Underneath it, of course, one remains as professional as ever and applies professional training, expertise and understanding within accepted and acceptable limits. Confident judgment is required. For instance, it is important to be able to distinguish the difference between a condescending feeling that parental and family contributions are less valid for being informal, and knowing that the family cannot help themselves. The outreach worker must get alongside the pupil and stick there, listening with active awareness, until the issues can be seen from their inside perspective. This is technique, not magic.

How to be effective

A reintegration programme is innovative. Any theoretical framework applied, including this working theory, will be incomplete, and subject to continuing improvement. *Every case generates a different picture, which calls for individual action to achieve its goals.*

The plan to which the outreach worker works must reflect comprehensively the educational, social and individual needs of the pupil. It needs not to be bound to a single approach or theory. A pragmatic attitude to effectiveness is preferable to the rigid adherence to a predetermined approach. (The requirement remains to act in the best interests of the client and in a way that is safe and properly monitored of course.) Behavioural reinforcement, for instance, is much more likely to be effective if the pupil is not aware that his or her behaviour has been reinforced. A pocketful of sweets, one of which is handed out from time to time, seemingly at random, is much more likely to change behaviour than tick charts and prizes which signal the intentions behind them.

The child understands his or her world and acts accordingly within a series of interlinked systems including home, school and peer group, as well as the wider societal context. This can be seen as a sort of 'ecosystem'. Any change in one part of the system will cause other parts to change correspondingly. The programme is therefore structurally inclusive, and an holistic approach is a requirement. Schools are seen as part of the community, just as are families and parents (and indeed the anarchic network of peer groups amongst which children move). *Parents are, effectively, co-professionals,* and the idiosyncratic aspects of their *modus operandi* are tolerated, accepted and respected just as those of any other agency must be.

Timing is of the essence. It is as if pupils are lurching from crisis to crisis. There will be points in the cycle at which real change in the 'ecosystem' can result in a spontaneous change in attitudes and behaviours on the part of the pupil. Crisis points may occur as events such as family conflicts or as part of dialogues, during which the rationale of the pupil or family members is being discussed. Someone needs to be there, at the 'fulcrum point', to offer a new interpretation of events, put forward or elicit a simple plan, and get people to commit to it. Staging meetings with plenty of advance warning in an unfamiliar environment which may be intimidating could be seen as less likely to produce results. Everyone practises their 'script' in advance, ensuring that they say and do the right things; but they may not be open at this testing time to the possibility of real change.

Whilst micro-changes in school function can be achieved (for instance changes in attitudes of key staff members leading to greater co-operation and a sympathetic approach), macro-changes in the system are beyond the remit of the pupil's outreach worker. Therefore some accommodation on the part of the pupil is required in accepting, and learning to function effectively within, the real-life constraints of an 'ordinary' school.

If there is to be a real partnership between schools, parents and pupils, then wherever possible the contributions of all members of a pupil's personal network should be recognised and valued, and their role does not end with having an opinion – they need to be able to own and commit to the strategies being suggested. *This will often mean that processes need to have a non-professional complexion, whilst the outreach worker ensures that they are professionally (i.e. effectively) delivered.*

Families automatically feel disenfranchised by the jargon and paraphernalia of formal meetings and reports. Likewise professionals need to rid themselves of the feeling that parental and family contributions are less valid for being informal. A good example is the typical reaction to a family group conference (FGC) plan. It is easy for professionals to see the flaws in the family's naive plans, and they are thus empowered to ignore them completely. What they miss is that the real difference is between their ability to see the flaws in the family's plan and their inability to see the flaws in their own. Acknowledgement by social services departments that placing a child in care carries its own risks is even now not universally accepted. However, it has no equivalence within education at all.

Many excluded children have been involved over some time with a succession of agencies. The outreach worker must liaise to ensure that the efforts of other professionals are not stampeded, and also be aware that any initiatives will be seen by their clients in the light of what other agencies have done. The pupil or their family may have more experience of professionals than the outreach worker. Sometimes this is used to manipulate situations, especially if there is a hidden agenda. Inasmuch as the work involves a form of counselling, the outreach worker should be 'unconditionally accepting, empathic, and congruent', as Carl Rogers

(1954) describes the process. This does not mean colluding with misdemeanours or avoiding unpalatable statements. But the idea is to get alongside the pupil and stick there, and this is best done by valuing and reflecting their imperatives whilst offering a sober and accurate assessment of the pupil's situation.

Outreach workers have to work with pupils and parents wherever and whenever they can. There is an on-going debate amongst psychologists as to whether the clinical or domestic setting is more appropriate for therapeutic work. The debate extends beyond the question of location to questions of confidentiality, boundaries and safety. Many adolescents pass through an anti-establishment phase and excluded children all the more so. Frequently, one or both parents of excluded children themselves had a difficult school life involving exclusion or special schooling, and may find institution settings difficult.

There is a reluctance on the part of many families to become further involved in what they see as a stigmatising experience. Visiting a 'clinic' reinforces the idea that 'treatment' is required for some sort of 'illness'. This is a view which they cannot uphold, because the inside perspective of the parents and the child strongly suggests otherwise. I generally ask the pupil and parents to make at least one visit to the office where I can administer profiling tools (see Chapter 6) and extend the assessment in a more formal setting. But this happens only after I have visited the home, and given the pupil and parents a chance to talk in their own terms on their own ground. After all, the task is to understand their 'ecosystem' and seek to become part of it in a way which allows the opportunity to bring about changes through the management of crisis. This is not going to be achieved by a hands-off approach. Once the initial two-way exchange of visits has been completed, meetings will take place by mutual agreement – in the office, at the home, sometimes at a parent's place of work, in cafés, or wherever else the people may be.

The outreach worker is therefore working with, and even within, the inside perspective of the personal network of the pupil, whilst interjecting an expert perspective in a non-judgmental way. By getting alongside the people concerned, he or she can bring together these perspectives and the perspective of the school and the teachers. There are numerous similarities between the mediating role of the peacemaker and a major point of the role of the outreach worker. The process must be therapeutic, not only in the way that the emotional damage to the pupil and the family is mitigated, but also in the sense of healing the educational damage, and remediating the failure of the pupil, the family, and the system.

6 Planning and assessment

Documenting the planning process

There are dangers in believing that a wholly mechanistic process of intervention will achieve the goal of real change. Figure 13 needs to be looked at in the context of everything that has been said up to this point about style, about engaging with the drama of childhood, about respecting and acknowledging the differing imperatives of the family, and about searching for the inside perspective of each person who is involved, from teachers to grannies. Each one of them collaborates on equal terms in the task of turning failure into success. If this is grasped, then Figure 13 will not be mistakenly seen as a graphic representation of the whole process, but simply as a useful mnemonic for planning out the one part of the change process which is not a soft change – the structure.

Referral information

Someone needs to draw together any relevant records for the outreach worker – this may seem obvious, and so it is. However, it is not unknown for relevant information not to be passed on and, in the case of permanently excluded children, for the whole school record to be re-routed into oblivion.

A competent outreach worker will not rely too heavily on 'the facts'. Although they provide useful starting points for exploration, they seldom form the basis for effective discussion because they do not in themselves provide clues as to the best way forward. *The outreach worker must focus on solutions, not problems.* Take the following report as an example:

> *Terry found the transition from primary school very difficult. He made a poor start at Thelma High School, presenting constantly challenging behaviour, being late for lessons, avoiding lessons, coming into conflict with peers, and being rude to staff. He had a one-day exclusion at the beginning of the Easter term, for rudeness to staff, and a five-day exclusion for fighting with a boy in*

Year 9, just before the end of the summer term. He appeared before the academic board a month ago and was given a final warning about his behaviour. The SEN Co-ordinator devised a plan which specified small achievable targets which Terry had helped to negotiate, but sadly he had another fight last week and is now awaiting permanent exclusion.

This report is a 'fact file', but it tells us almost nothing about what is really going on for Terry, and what we can do about it. Discussing the fights will not help much, either, since he may well have forgotten why they happened in the first place. In fact, he may not even understand why he got angry enough to start hitting people. Where is the report of a conversation with mother and other family members? Why did the transition from primary school go so badly? Has he started puberty yet? Here is a much more useful report:

Terry got into fights on the two mornings after his dad, whom he has not seen for 18 months, failed to turn up to take him out as promised. His dad always

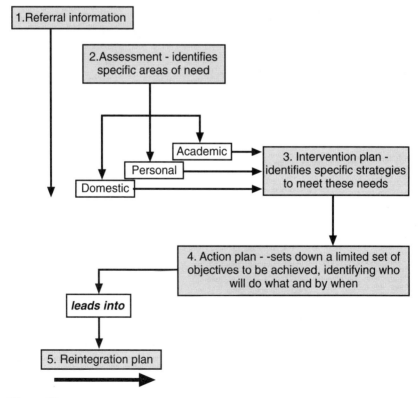

Figure 13

does this, saying he will take Terry out, but then not show up. The boys he fought were both at his primary school. One used to be picked up by his dad in a Jaguar. The other was always teasing Terry about doing his mum's shopping. Oh yes, mum has a bit of an alcohol problem, and was once seen lying on the grass in the school playground, 'resting'.

This sort of report is worth its weight in diamonds, and can be obtained only by using a different approach to information gathering. The more usual sort of report is worth having as a baseline, so long as 'the facts' do not obstruct the search for the real story. The second report is also incomplete, of course, because lots of boys are let down by their parents and do not start fights. So the outreach worker will need to further assess the pupil.

There are hard facts which it is really useful to have, such as accurate data on literacy and numeracy. Surprisingly, this information may be difficult to obtain as well. For instance, the school records may contain a reading test – but it turns out to be over a year old. Sometimes the 'facts' about attainment conflict or seem unlikely. Another pupil who was supposed to be behind in all subjects actually achieved at least average attainment levels in six out of eight subjects. A third pupil appeared never to have taken a Maths assessment! A Ghanaian pupil who was supposed to have learning difficulties turned out to be trilingual; being able to converse in Swahili and Ga was not, apparently, considered a significant skill!

For all these reasons it is no good relying on the standard sort of referral information alone: a detailed assessment is required.

Assessment

Figure 13 identifies three domains for assessment: domestic, individual and academic. The boundaries between them are not going to be absolute – there will be overlap. Figure 14 picks out some problems with excluded children and some common approaches to satisfying their needs.

Remember that the exercise is an assessment of needs, not problems. When problems are reconstructed as needs, the terminology changes so that misdemeanours are displaced by concerns. The emphasis in the solutions then becomes support and development, rather than control and punishment.

This difference arises directly from the kind of information being gathered. The example of the referral information given above illustrates this point.

- *Domestic assessment.* The word 'domestic' is used, rather than 'family', because there may be relevant elements in the pupil's out-

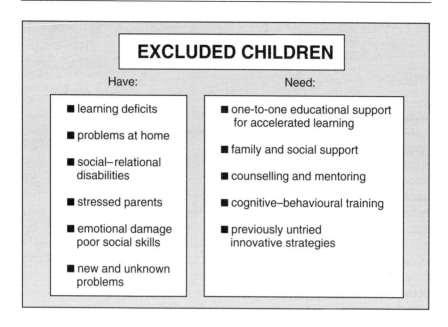

Figure 14

of-school life which extend beyond immediate family, such as neighbours and family friends. 'Domestic' also implies something about the home economy and environment.

■ *Individual assessment.* The assessment of the pupil as an individual includes aspects of psychology, lifestyle, personal health and habits, attitudes and outlook. For older children there may be an out-of-school peer group which has an impact. However, for assessment purposes this group may not be very useful. Even members of the group do not know what is going on in the group. Adolescent relationships are anarchic, rapidly changing and secretive.

■ *Academic assessment.* It is frequently the case that pupils who come into conflict with schools are of above-average ability, but underachieving. In fact, this is the classic rule-of-thumb used in assessing · children for an SEN Statement which identifies 'emotional and behavioural difficulties' requiring 'a school where children can be taught in small groups and their therapeutic needs addressed' (Statement code for 'EBD school'). Sometimes the pupil is not underachieving, but is causing problems for the teachers. So the academic assessment really consists of two parts – the academic attainments of the pupils, and teacher information about classroom behaviour, attitudes and approach to learning, and so on. Out-of-class in-school behaviour can be seen as forming part of the academic assessment or the personal assessment.

Reassessment will be necessary from time to time. One way of taking an on-the-job audit is to ask oneself whether professionals have got enough of a 'handle' on the case: something which makes it easy to grasp, although not necessarily which provides a simple solution. For instance, one handle in Aleem's case (Appendix 1) was that he was extremely anxious about his mother's health (with some justification). This anxiety was driving him homeward during the day, through the mechanism of phantom illness or misdemeanours carrying an 'exclusion tariff'. Here was a clearly defined and simple causal link which made his case comparatively easy to move forward. Apparently, no-one in his previous school knew this, and his school records made no mention of it.

A core dynamic of successful reintegration work is the discovery of previously concealed information which makes sense of the pupil's difficulties. Induction is only complete when the outreach worker has got to this level of understanding, and this can take some time.

Peter was a 10-year-old boy who had been permanently excluded from his primary school, and his case had been referred to a special reintegration programme. The reasons given by the school for excluding him were that his behaviour was often silly and disruptive, he was disobedient, and he sometimes ran out of the school gates and would not return. The school felt they had an excellent case on safety grounds for permanently excluding him. However, at a meeting with school staff and management it became clear that their commitment to difficult pupils was very low. He was a very difficult boy to get hold of, frequently failing to attend meetings. His parents were either also out, or they just said he had gone out and they did not know when he would return. The situation bordered on grounds for social services referral. However, he was obviously streetwise and usually with friends, so no referral was made. His parents were asked to attend meetings but never managed to make it. The temptation to send a curt letter asking for an explanation, or to refer the case on, was strong. There was pressure from line managers to make something happen; but the question was – what? On one occasion, Peter's father (also called Peter but known as 'Pete') phoned up half an hour before the meeting and said: 'We really do want to have a meeting, we are definitely coming, we are on our way.' They still did not make it, and it became clear that something beyond their control was stopping them. I guessed it was something to do with the baggage Pete was carrying regarding authority, school and teachers.

I switched tacks, going round to the house once again and finding his mother in. She suggested that I try in the local pub. Sure enough, there Pete was with his mates, and we settled down to a game of pool and a pint of beer. One of his friends let slip that he had just come out of prison. Pete said: 'Maureen said I should tell you, but I didn't want to.' Once the cat was out of the bag, he opened up completely.

Pete was a local 'villain'. He was a pleasant enough chap, who obviously had quite an image to keep up. When he needed transport, he just made one call on the mobile, and his driver was there. He had been in trouble and 'inside' on numerous occasions. I did not ask for the details. Peter idolised his dad, and had been badly affected by his father's occasional disappearances. This was one of many losses. Apart from the deaths of his great grandparents, both grandmothers had died in the space of a few years. Both had been instrumental in his upbringing and their loss would have had quite an impact on Peter's day-to-day life. Finally, his uncle had died suddenly from a blood clot only a few weeks before. He knew that the underlying causes 'ran in the family' and that his mother had the same problem. The strain on his family had led to a breakdown in normally supportive relationships, so Peter and Maureen were now estranged from the rest of the family, although Pete and his younger sister were still able to visit from time to time. Oh yes, Pete's father was also dying of cancer.

To say that this catalogue of woes was making Peter anxious would be an understatement. Any 10-year-old is likely to be trying to come to terms with the universality of death. Peter was also trying to adjust to the numerous deaths of people he loved very much. However, on top of this, he knew that people can die suddenly (such as his uncle) and that his father might be arrested at any time. Who would look after him then?

All this information was obtained only because I had been willing to go to the pub and have a drink with my client. The rest followed naturally. I had 'joined' with Pete, and made it clear to him that we could meet on his terms, not just on mine. The professional boundary was still there, but it was internalised. Once the facts were out in the open, the action plan was obvious. Peter needed bereavement counselling and that is what he got. The family also needed a great deal of support. The head teacher of a local primary school offered him a place, having enough insight to realise that Peter's problems were manageable, and that he was safer in school than out.

Gathering information

Where to meet

There is no quicker way of getting a three-dimensional picture of the pupils than to see the home environment first-hand. It also creates a unique instant bond between the pupil and the outreach worker, and if the outreach worker also happens to be a teacher at the school it makes it much easier to adopt a different role. But the best reason for meeting at the home is that it is likely to be the place the parent feels safest, strongest and most confident. It is a great environment in which to share confidences as well.

Once a home meeting has taken place, it is much less daunting for parents and pupils to visit a school office or other professional centre, where more business-like aspects of the assessment process can take place. Office appointments are much more likely to be missed, and if they do not work, then the outreach worker should simply do the business in the home at a second or third visit. It is quite a good idea not to do business on the first meeting: form-filling, technicalities and note-taking will obstruct the building of a relationship. What does the client see when the professional is fiddling with clip-files crammed with officialese, or trying to track down the 'right' bit of paper? Is the professional fully aware of the client and surrounding?

Explaining yourself

When the outreach worker makes initial contact with the family, the question arises: 'Who are you?'. Whatever the outreach worker's usual role – teacher, welfare officer, social worker, or psychologist – for the purposes of this work he or she is simply a reintegration or outreach worker. Actually this role carries no statutory powers, and has no official status. This is very much in its favour. It may or may not be appropriate to make the kind of declaration shown on page 102, but something similar would be good. For those who are not known previously to the family but do have a professional status, the statement could be prefaced by something like this:

> *Some of the time I work for the Department of Psychology, but in this job I am just an outreach worker. I'm not ... [etc.]*

If the outreach worker is already known to the pupil and family one needs to say something like:

> *You know me from school as your class tutor/head-of-year, but for now I am just here as an outreach worker. I'm not ... [etc.]*

Sometimes contact is difficult. Basic information such as contact phone numbers must be collected now, or at the first home visit. When is the best time to phone? Do they work, and if so can you contact them there? Can they phone out easily? Are there working or other time restrictions on meeting or talking opportunities? How can you avoid conflicting with other domestic demands? By tactfully eliciting this sort of information you are helping them to practise disclosure, you are showing that you understand there might be difficulties for them, and that you empathise. Have you given them a contact number for evening calls? One little secret revealed in many cases is that poor families can have incoming calls only – for obvious reasons. This is sometimes a source of embarrassment. It is so easy to say 'Can you call me', and then later 'How unreliable!' when they do not call. But calling out actually means going to the phone box – not always easy to do. Have you shown that you trust them by revealing something personal about yourself? *Giving trust earns trust.*

The outreach worker should exude confidence and an easy-going friendliness. This is the time to:

- declare your commitment to the inclusion of the pupil and their success in school;

- clearly request the assistance of carers;

- ask the pupil to confirm that he or she wants to go back to school;

- ask to be told in the pupil's own words what went wrong;

- ask the parents to contribute their views;

- acknowledge explicitly the validity of their versions of events.

Explain that you want to get the best possible picture of the situation so that you can help the pupil and the family; explain that you want to get a handle on the situation and ask them to come to your base for a second meeting; explain your child protection policy to them (see Appendix 2). The difficulties of reintegration should not be minimised (quite the reverse); but you can confirm that, if they will work with you, together you can make it happen. You have the know-how but it will be up to the pupil to achieve it. Ask the pupil to confirm again that he or she wants to do this. Above all, the past becomes history – this is the beginning of the new beginning. At every step:

- explain;

- challenge;

- encourage.

Winning the trust of carers or pupils is much more than a matter of being nice. Yes, you must show them you care about people, you like them, and you have the expertise required. You know they need help, and they are very likely to want to confide and seek moral support. In this context your liking should become genuine. If it does not, then either you are not doing the job, or you are not cut out for it. But trust works both ways. Will you give them your home phone number? If not, why not? Both pupils and family referred to me get the home phone number and the mobile number. In the many years in which I have been giving out my number, only one client has misused this confidence, calling me (on one occasion) at 3am on a Sunday morning.

Just as, according to Karl Marx, differences in wealth alienate people from each other, so do differences in culture and power. One victim of this alienation is trust, and trust cannot automatically follow liking. For trust to develop there must be liking, equality of power, and common ground. Easy assumptions about access or neutral ground may be very misguided. For instance, if a journey requires a fare to be paid, does the parent have any money? Believe it or not, the answer can be:

'I'm really sorry, I couldn't come to the meeting today. The giro arrives tomorrow and until then I don't have a penny.'

If the parent is too embarrassed to admit this sort of thing, confusion can result.

Meeting in a local café may seem like a sensible way to find neutral ground, and anyway you are looking forward to having a great cappuccino at that little Italian place. Unfortunately, to your client this is a strange and self-conscious environment. You might as well be meeting at the local GU clinic! If you ask them to nominate a place they might suggest McDonald's. Going along with their line of least resistance shows you are trusting them, and makes it much easier for them to start trusting you.

As quickly as possible, any other members of the team on this case, and teachers and support workers (such as mentors, counsellors or befrienders), should make their first contacts and begin to form an alternative view, from their perspectives. Teachers and support workers can provide a subject- or expertise-specific informal assessment (together with their impressions of home life). A decision will need to be made as early as possible as to whether a formal education assessment needs to be conducted. If specific learning programmes such as SRA (Science Research Associates) accelerated literacy are going to be used, the appropriate assessment scheme (there is usually a programme entry assessment) should be administered.

▉ 'Individual' assessment

Many people instinctively mistrust questionnaires and inventories. They are rightly concerned that the information could be used in a mechanistic way. They dislike the idea of reducing a human life to a histogram or number. They do not necessarily find them revealing.

I share all these concerns. Many psychological assessment tools require special training to use. However, there are also many that are simple and easily understood. Any competent professional can administer them, and the real skill comes in how the results are interpreted.

It is really up to the administrator to decide how the data will be interpreted and its use should be limited by their usefulness. Sometimes the data is very revealing (for instance, see Raymond's story in Appendix 1), but if it is not then it can be ignored. In particular, there is no obligation to calculate a score – although this might prove valuable in evaluating some aspects of the programme as a whole. The individual items of a questionnaire may be treated as statements. If one seems important, it is an obvious first step to seek confirmation and clarification directly from the respondent.

Inventories have many qualities which make them very functional for the task of gathering information:

- They ask questions comprehensively.

- They do so quickly.

- People find them relatively easy, and even fun, to do.

- People often find it easier to tick a box to indicate a problem than to write it down or say out loud what the problem is.

- It is less irritating to answer one question after another using tick boxes.

- People may forget there is a particular problem until prompted.

- The questionnaire is neutral and appears non-judgmental.

You can preface the administration of a questionnaire with a statement like:

> *Now, I know most of these questions will not apply to you. This questionnaire is designed for very young children as well, and with much more serious difficulties than your child. So just tick the 'never' box and carry on.*

Parents and pupils generally find the process of ticking boxes less intimidating and soon settle down. The range and variety of positive responses may be surprising. If you are not going to use inventories or questionnaires, how are you going to gather information comprehensively in an efficient and inoffensive manner?

The instruments listed below are ones that I have found useful. Other instruments I have used from time to time include ones for depression and anger.

It is beyond the scope of this book to detail the rationale, method and interpretation of each one. Interested readers should research their own approach to assessment using the references provided and their own expertise, with help from local departments of psychiatry or psychology. These links will also help to create a network of *ad hoc* advisory and collaborative sources.

Achenbach's Child Behaviour Checklist (CBCL)

This checklist has a number of questions on social activity, and just over 100 short questions, not limited to behaviour, which can be answered in about half an hour (Achenbach, 1974). I also find it useful in generating a profile across a number of 'internalised' and 'externalised' personality aspects (such as 'attention problems', 'anxiety' and 'withdrawn'). Achenbach stresses that the objective is not to generate labels but to provides a means of summarising human diversity. He stresses the need to back up the CBCL with field observations and other data.

The CBCL comes in three versions: for parent, teacher and pupil. It is therefore conveniently possible to compare the perspectives of these three parties against a common set of questions.

Speilberger's State–Trait Anxiety Inventory

This is a short anxiety inventory (Speilberger, 1973). I use only the 'trait' section – i.e. anxiety as a characteristic of the individual rather than as a state of mind in response to recent events. I have used both total score and high-scoring individual items as indicators of problem areas worth exploring with a family or pupil.

Coopersmith's Self-Esteem Inventory

This is a short self-esteem inventory (Coopersmith, 1991). 'Self-esteem' is a term much used in education, and many people seem to be able to identify low self-esteem easily. However, it is much more difficult to evaluate than might seem to be the case. Ruth Wylie (1974) identified three quite different constructs which might be called self-esteem. She said that self-esteem might be:

- what I tell people I think of myself;
- what I believe I really think of myself;
- what my feelings about myself really are.

It is easy to spot the first one being expressed. It is not difficult, when using this inventory, to spot the 'right' answer, and when people make 'perfect' scores they are probably being defensive about themselves. This is revealing in itself. Nevertheless, the individual items in this inventory can be valuable, particularly if there are very few negative items. When John (see Appendix 1) completed this inventory the first time there was only one item about which he could not decide whether the statement was 'like me' or 'unlike me': the item was 'My family understands me'. At the end of the programme he knew the answer was 'like me'.

Semi-structured interviews

I also use a semi-structured interview (that is, one with specific questions, from which open-ended enquiry may follow) which is based on a simple model of non-attendance. Exclusion seems so often to be a non-attendance strategy in which, although the circumstances are different, the root causes are often similar. Parents and other family members may be interviewed, and this could involve additional visits, at various locations.

Other agency involvement

In order to set out in collaboration rather than in conflict with other agencies, it is essential to canvas the views of those known to have been recently involved with the pupil, and agree an 'interagency strategy'. Often no other agencies are involved, and equally often their involvement is nominal. When the outreach worker demonstrates a determination to engage with the case other professionals are often very positive. They are glad someone else is doing something, and an agreement to liaise and communicate, as necessary, is often sufficient. Where an agency such as social services is substantially involved, it is highly likely that their immediate concern will be for aspects other than education, although there could still be overlap of approach. In this case a meeting may be advisable to co-ordinate plans.

The involvement of an alternative education organisation (such as a therapeutic centre) or any formal statutory involvements can create the potential for conflicts of interest which must be dealt with separately. The process described in the following pages may need to be modified or curtailed, for instance because of statutory requirements.

From assessment to planning

The plan has two parts: the intervention plan and the action plan. They are closely linked. The main difference is that the intervention plan relates needs to strategies, and the action plan relates strategies to action. By the end of the third week it should be possible to collate any of the following which have been collected:

- historical reports;

- any interagency strategy needed;

- one-to-one teacher's and support worker's observations and assessments;

- family's and pupil's views;

- a formal education assessment if required;

- teachers' and senior managers' views.

Either one or two planning meetings can be held (depending on how proactive the family are). Out of this by agreement will come a comprehensive plan, written in plain language, which specifies the pupil's role and educational needs, and the family's role, as well as any psychosocial concerns.

This may sound a bit like the statutory assessment process, in which multidisciplinary views are gathered and a plan devised. *There is a huge difference in approach, in flexibility, and in management.* The approach has been described in this book already. The statutory process, which is due for revision, is too ponderous and mechanistic. Greater flexibility can be achieved by utilising the untapped potential of committed professionals, who will use their understanding and experience to provide a comprehensive and sufficient assessment, drawing on other agencies only when necessary. Finally, the management of the process lies in the hands of the outreach worker, who can make immediate executive decisions, rather than a local authority department which is obliged to use a hands-off approach.

REINTEGRATION PLAN (PART 1)

Planning sheet for ___Aleem___ date ___Oct. 10. 97___

What needs doing?	How is it going to get done?	Who is going to do it?	What do they need?
Modern languages weakness & dislike	Regular weekly x2 sessions with Clare Read to A.A. at weekly session	C.A. A.A.	J'ecoute! Parts I - II Copies of current work
Maintain forward momentum in learning	6 sessions per wk. with English & Maths	J.M. T.S.	Teacher to supply from archives
? Speech impediment	Speech therapy via GP A.A. to write letter, mum to take	A.A. Mum	Letter from A.A.
? Anxieties about Mum during school day	Investigate use of pager so that mum can confirm everything is OK Planning & funding needed	A.A.	A.A. to investigate
? Self-esteem & independence	One week respite stay on Norfolk farm — end of November	Via E.A. homes prog.	Funding from John Smith Foundation
Self-management skills	One per week role-play & modelling session	T.S.	Good attendance

Plan agreed by ___Aleem Yusuf___ ___J. Yusuf___

ALEEM YUSUF   JENNIFER YUSUF   ADAM ABDELNOOR

Figure 15

The plan does not need to be elaborate and will certainly be drafted on a single sheet of paper. This plan is agreed with pupil and family who then sign a contract with the outreach worker in which they commit themselves to its success. Each objective in the plan also needs to be written down in a column, and alongside it should appear the initials of the person who is to achieve it, and how they intend to do this (obviously a clear literacy learning goal, for instance, may have a more focused course content than a social objective to do with family relationships). Later the outcome can be recorded, and further or amended goals then justified.

In an ideal world, this process would be completed on time and in every respect. Although things do not work out quite like that, the basic structure does need to be in place even if it does not look like the above. The key features are:

- an inclusive style, bringing together all parties, both family and professional;

- equal consideration given to educational, personal and domestic issues;

- a sharing and loving attitude shown by staff to their clients;

- needs linked to specific actions through appropriate and effective strategies.

The types of plan which work are shown by the case studies recorded in Appendix 1. Figure 15 shows an example of 'concrete planning', whereby everyone knows exactly what they are supposed to be doing, and how. There are no vague intentions, nor woolly expectations.

Normally a course of treatment or a plan is reviewed and a revised plan is devised based on the review. This is relatively easy when the pupil is still in full-time attendance, although sufficient time must be allowed for interventions to work. In more serious cases where a pupil has been excluded for a longer term, or permanently, things are more difficult. The outreach worker might like to review the results of the action plan that has been implemented before beginning the return to school. If a pupil and family have invested in the process of restructuring in a committed way, there are perhaps grounds for optimism that the programme has achieved its objectives. However, the effect of any interventions can only truly be judged within the real-life context of a new school. Using threshold criteria might help (see Chapter 8).

7 Choosing the right strategies for intervention

The choice of strategy is driven by what will be effective in a particular case. There is a tendency for professionals to become skilled in a particular technique and then apply it to every case. However practical this might be on a cost, skills and resources basis, it is not needs-led, and is bound to fail in some cases. Naturally enough, the next step is to decide that the family or pupil are too dysfunctional or downright oppositional! Every service and every organisation is ultimately dependent on the competencies of its personnel – professionals will become more competent if they are given more opportunity to become multi-skilled and operate in a flexible environment.

A recent review of ten successful reintegration cases revealed the following:

- In nine cases, pupils were referred before term 3 of Year 9.

- Both the pupil and the outreach worker were male in each case.

- There were high levels of empathy towards the pupil and family members, and a corresponding level of trust and confidence in the project manager.

- The families were able to disclose relevant information.

- A conscious and determined attempt was made to empower the family.

- Pupils were treated with obvious respect, but were also strongly and assertively directed.

- A thorough and 'three-dimensional' assessment was carried out, based upon the use of analytical instruments, and incorporating the 'clients' perspective'.

- Problem behaviours or concerns were seen as being meaningful within this perspective, and specific interventions were made to address the issues arising from this understanding.

- Generally, these interventions were concrete, practical initiatives.

- Where counselling was provided, this was always in support of other interventions.

- Advice and mentoring was a core element of the project.

- Respite break opportunities of from three to ten days in a rural setting were enjoyed by half the pupils in the sample.

- Self-management skills were important.

- Advice and mentoring for parents was provided to some degree in all cases.

- Specific literacy programmes and specific numeracy programmes were provided in the 40 per cent of cases where the pupils' attainment levels in either were seriously undermining their progress.

- Study and learning skills were a specific element of 60 per cent of individual programmes.

- In a few cases pupils had specific extracurricular activities such as a motorbike maintenance and riding group.

- All pupils were coached in modifying their behaviour – mainly by cognitive and strategic interventions. A formal behaviour modification programme was viewed as appropriate for only a minority of pupils.

Getting a handle on the situation

Plans are much more likely to succeed if they are grounded in the real world, and there is a sense of ownership on the part of the main players – the pupil, the parents and the outreach worker. Above all the outreach worker must establish grounds for a few pivotal issues, around which determined effort can coalesce. Inspiration is required to bring these issues into focus. Once established they are like the handles which everyone can grasp. They are almost always simple direct assertions which have a ring of truth to them.

The planning process can go on even if no-one has a handle on the situation. However, the plan will then need to be very much about how the outreach worker is going to set about getting a handle on the situation! Very often, the solutions lie with the family, and the bonds must be given time to form before the family is able to share their insights, which are very often the cause of guilt or shame. Equally often, the outreach worker can reflect on the pupil's predicament, using their own experience and understanding of child development to identify the pivotal issues quickly and easily.

The concerns that arise from this planning process are in each case unique, and the methods used for addressing them are either specific programmes or courses designed to adapt to specific needs (such as a particular literacy programme), or 'one-off' strategies of varying ingenuity. There are an extraordinary number of different approaches to therapy: cognitive training, behaviour modification, accelerated learning, specific learning difficulty, family work, peer work, youth work, reducing delinquency and crime, community initiatives, etc. Many of them are locally based and unevaluated; and although many of them are effective where they are delivered by committed workers, they are not formally reported and their discovery and dissemination is haphazard. Sutton (1996) concludes that, amongst other things, activities that 'engage with the offender's thinking' and techniques that include 'modelling, graduated practice, rehearsal, role-play, reinforcement, resource provision and cognitive restructuring' are more likely to work.

Anyone carrying out this work will bring their own expertise to it, or borrow from others. The outreach worker does not need to be able to deliver all aspects of the programme as long as someone in the team can. The plan will identify education, and domestic and personal concerns; if some aspect is beyond the scope of the programme personnel, then another agency will need to be involved.

Problem children who merit exclusion deserve to be dealt with seriously, but what that means depends on the perspective. There are reasonably cost-competitive solutions that adopt an ethical and humane approach to the problem, in line with government thinking on inclusion, the SEN *Code of Practice*, and high professional and educational standards.

In families of excluded pupils the deficits are multiple and rectifiable. The exciting word in that statement is the last one, but the key word is 'multiple'. When problems cross agency boundaries how is assistance to be provided in a fair, effective and professionally rigorous way? This book is an attempt to find an answer to the question of multiagency and multidisciplinary working within an acceptable budget. Cost, though, is not the only question. The need to cross professional boundaries creates its own difficulties: one study found that where agencies collaborated, most of the time was spent sharing information (Joseph Rowntree Foundation, 1994). Meetings are time-consuming and generate their own work. Interagency conflicts, which often arise, are undermining for all concerned.

It is simply not realistic to have more than one agency working with a family, unless there is agreement as to which agencies are in a subsidiary role. From the families' point of view multiple agency involvement means extra meetings where the same ground is gone over again and again, and long delays during which nothing appears to be happening. In terms of 'sharing the problem', it is all too easy for parents to bond to the 'wrong' professional, disclosing information and generally opening up, willing to be guided and receive help. If the professional concerned is unwilling to deal with the problem and simply refers on, 'disclosure fatigue' may set in, and parental apathy (often in the face of inordinate delay) takes over. It is not unusual for cases to be transferred between professionals,and although this may move things on, it often arises from institutional pressures which have nothing to do with the case itself. In a fragmented situation, any further fragmentation may undermine any changes for the better.

This is starkly highlighted by the educational needs of children in care, where social services and education should have been able to collaborate in what is a well-defined and stable area. The poor quality of the information about their educational circumstances is a symptom of the difficulties both agencies have in sharing responsibility and management for this group. The permanent exclusion rate among children in care is ten times higher than the average; perhaps as many as 30 per cent of children in care are out of mainstream education, whether through exclusion or truancy. As the government's Social Exclusion Unit report (1998) says:

> Some of this may be attributable to poor communication between professionals. Studies have shown that social services staff are often vague about the exclusion status of children in their care or how to appeal and that schools do not always know that a child is in care. ... A new placement in a new area disrupts education through a change of school. Exclusion can add to this vicious circle: many foster parents cannot cope with a child at a loose end all day, so exclusion often triggers a breakdown in care placement.

There are a number of programmes available to professionals which can claim a degree of success in alleviating social dysfunction, such as intensive home visiting of young mothers, skills training for delinquents, pre-school enrichment programmes, parent management training, programmes for reducing socioeconomic deprivation, peer mentoring, and in-school programmes (Farrington, 1996). More recent approaches involve partnerships with non-teaching professionals, performance coaching (where the emphasis is on removing the 'interference' of negative and distracting thoughts and feelings), and distinction-based learning (encouraging pupils to recognise and explore a greater range of opportunities – see Appendix 3).

The difficulties arise in justifying their implementation within a strategic framework. Sceptics argue that there is little statistical evidence in support of such programmes, although it is fully recognised by the academic community that the kind of evidence they demand is notoriously difficult to collect. Authorities and agencies do not trust small independent teams operating idiosyncratically, although these may often be more successful because the professionals involved find autonomy motivating, and make good use of the freedom to be flexible.

In an effort to gather the kind of monitoring information that would justify this sort of programme to the sceptics, and ensure centralised control, an administrative bureaucracy is set up which often serves only to divert energy away from practice and into paperwork. Furthermore, this inflates the cost of implementation, decreasing the cost-effectiveness of the programme.

The Audit Commission's 1996 report, called *Misspent Youth: Young People and Crime*, identifies common qualities of successful young-offender programmes. Whilst the specific examples they give may not be not relevant to excluded pupils, the general observations may be. Programmes should have clear, skills-oriented goals, and apply cognitive –behavioural methods, based on real-life learning in the community. Just as the Audit Commission points out that specific factors lead to offending, so specific factors lead to exclusion, and these should be dealt with separately from educational needs. The programme needs to be focused on employment (i.e. school-focused). The active participation of the client is required within a carefully structured programme. Finally, the level of intervention needs to match the level of risk of re-offending (i.e. re-exclusion).

The Audit Commission found that general individual or family counselling, psychodynamic therapy, unstructured groups, and punishment did not appear to work. Since the use of counselling approaches cropped up in earlier chapters, it is worth emphasising that the authors of the report were dismissive not of the approaches themselves, but of their use in a general sort of way. Programmes with aims (such as 'increase self-esteem' or 'focus on emotional and personal problems') but not goals (typified by clear demonstrable objectives and localised involvement) were much less successful, as were programmes which simply addressed neighbourhood living conditions without addressing individual needs.

Figure 16 shows some of the range of possible interventions that may be employed as strategies in working with young people at risk of school failure. The lists are not exhaustive. Sometimes practical solutions do not seem to fit into any category or type. Anyone carrying out this kind of work will bring their own expertise to it, or even 'borrow' the expertise of others. It may seem unrealistic to expect to find anyone with such an array of skills; however, if professionals are given the opportunity to

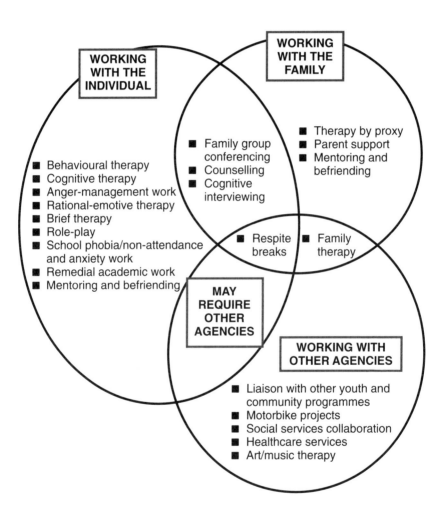

Figure 16

work creatively, flexibly and expansively, it is surprising how quickly the skills base develops. After all, the challenge is to find affordable ways of delivering effective services. If this did not present a difficulty, then services would already be providing it.

The various strategies are grouped into three domains: working with individuals, working with families, and strategies which always require other agencies to be involved. The figure is drawn from the point of view of the outreach worker, regardless of whether the outreach worker is employed by the school or by another organisation. 'Other agencies' are agencies in addition to the one carrying out the reintegration work. Their involvement will mean that some sort of interagency strategy becomes necessary. Generally, these additional interventions are stand-alone strategies aimed at specific needs such as speech therapy. Depending on the competencies of the outreach worker, other agencies might get involved with any part of the plan.

Working with individuals and families

It would be unrealistic to expect a school to be able to resource every technique described below. Nevertheless it should be helpful to have an overview of what each one involves so that informed decisions can be made. A brief description will be given of each, together with a more detailed description of several approaches schools could adopt with relative ease. More information appears in Appendix 3.

Working with individuals

Therapy is a word that alarms some people and turns others off. People may assume that all therapy is psychoanalytical, and even visualise a Freudian style scenario in which the patient lies on a *chaise longue* with the inevitably male and bearded therapist just behind. However, some confusion is perfectly understandable, given the recent proliferation of therapies. The ones specifically highlighted in this chapter reflect the important elements in facilitating change in pupils.

Behavioural therapy

Behavioural therapy (also known as behaviour modification) programmes should utilise small, frequent and immediate rewards for behaviours that are frequently repeated. It seldom works to use a major event such as a holiday as a big reward for long-term changes in activity because the connection between action and reward is often lost, and the stakes are just too high. Are you really going to deny a pupil a respite break because he missed his behaviour target of 90 per cent positive tuition reports over half a term? What will this achieve? Far better to give him an immediate reward like a sweet or drink intermittently and on a random basis when he turns up for sessions, without even telling him his behaviour is being reinforced!

Pupils are not pigeons in a cage, and if they think they are being treated as such they will simply not perform. Younger children may enjoy keeping tick charts, adding up points and achieving various targets which entitle them to rewards. If they do so, it is likely to be for reasons which are not behavioural at all, but simply because they have made decisions about making others and themselves happy. If, unusually, a formal behaviour modification programme is considered, it should be with the co-operation and consent of family and pupil. This would apply where a pupil was very clear about specific behaviours or reactions over which he or she wanted to have control, but recognised that was not the case. On such occasions it might be worth referring to a behavioural psychologist, who can apply greater experience to the task of devising ingenious behavioural training.

Where school phobia or anxiety is dealt with by a prompt return to school the process is sometimes known as 'flooding'. This is a behavioural technique by which aversive stimuli are presented in full strength during which the facilitator is able to monitor, manage and ameliorate aversive reactions to them. Some reactions extinguish themselves spontaneously, others can be mitigated by a more cognitive approach. Similarly, when an arachnophobe is required to hold a spider in the hand, aversive reaction is soon mediated. Expectations that the feeling will be horrible are replaced by the discovery that the spider is so light that its touch is unfelt. Nor does it run as fast as the arachnophobe expects, and so on.

The same effect can be obtained in a gradual way – instead of putting a spider on the hand straight away, it is introduced by way of talking about baby spiders, looking at pictures, holding pictures, holding a small spider in a glass box, and so on. All the time the therapist is providing positive and relaxing stimuli such as tranquil music, praise and reward. The process relies upon the psychological phenomenon that responses to positively conditioned stimuli tend to take precedence over responses to negatively conditioned stimuli. The overall effect is to recondition the response to the negative stimuli – in the end the stimuli that triggered an aversive response start to trigger a positive one.

Cognitive–behavioural therapy

Cognitive–behavioural programmes are different from behaviour modification, because behaviour is changed not through the application of rewards and sanctions, but by the mediation of new ways of thinking, which in turn (at least in theory) promotes new ways of feeling.

Cognitive–behavioural therapy may best be viewed as a class of strategies that involve working on thinking as it affects behaviour.

A general model of thinking and behaviour is shown in Figure 17. It is not a single type of procedure – cognitive behavioural psychologists seek

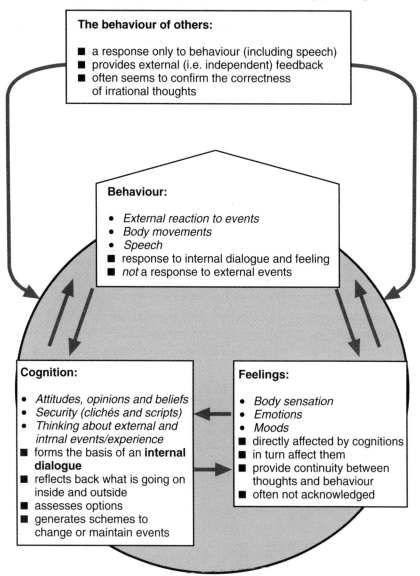

The behaviour of others:

- ■ a response only to behaviour (including speech)
- ■ provides external (i.e. independent) feedback
- ■ often seems to confirm the correctness of irrational thoughts

Behaviour:

- • *External reaction to events*
- • *Body movements*
- • *Speech*
- ■ response to internal dialogue and feeling
- ■ *not* a response to external events

Cognition:

- • *Attitudes, opinions and beliefs*
- • *Security (clichés and scripts)*
- • *Thinking about external and intrnal events/experience*
- ■ forms the basis of an **internal dialogue**
- ■ reflects back what is going on inside and outside
- ■ assesses options
- ■ generates schemes to change or maintain events

Feelings:

- • *Body sensation*
- • *Emotions*
- • *Moods*
- ■ directly affected by cognitions
- ■ in turn affect them
- ■ provide continuity between thoughts and behaviour
- ■ often not acknowledged

Figure 17

to apply theory on a situational or even individual case basis. Two examples are treatment for school phobia (e.g. Blagg, 1987) and anger-management programmes (e.g. Novaco, 1975).

Nigel Blagg was able to achieve a high rate of return to school amongst primary-phase children. First he constructed a simple model for explaining non-attendance at school. For individual children, he identified precipitating factors either at school or at home (or both) which, taken together, led to a school phobic episode. This is the cognitive aspect. The behavioural response was that the child stayed away from school. As a result maintaining factors arose, which together with the facilitating factors added up to another school phobic episode (or continued absence). The solution was to break into the cognitive component and change it, and at the same time to alter the maintaining behaviour. Blagg's four-step plan was as follows:

1. Clarify the problem (what happened, when, why, on-going fears, etc.).

2. Desensitise the worries of child and parent, by providing new 'scripts' to replace the old 'can't do' clichés and reasoning.

3. Plan for all contingencies (how the behavioural aspects will be managed, what if child tries to return home, etc.).

4. Persuade the parents to co-operate in ensuring a quick and complete return to school (physically managing attendance, child must continue to attend, parents must enforce, etc.).

This strategy lies more on the behavioural side, and Novaco's anger-management programme lies more on the cognitive side. Novaco first enlists the commitment of the 'client', by ensuring that he or she recognises the need to change. This is a first step, without which the programme cannot function. It is in effect a coaching programme in which clients learn the model shown in Figure 17. They then go on to understand how their own behaviour fits into it. In particular they learn how their angry outbursts (behaviour) relate to their failure to monitor their own feelings and to cultivate unhealthy ones, and their tendency to run unhelpful 'scripts' or hold unhelpful attitudes and beliefs. Finally, they are given a programme designed to change their thinking, increase their awareness of healthy feelings, and help them avoid unhealthy ones.

Cognitive therapies also reappear under other guises as *solution-focused therapy* or *brief therapy*. Both are more recent methods for quickly and effectively changing thinking and behaviour. They suit young people who are not inclined to engage in too much regular introspection. It helps if you can get the message across while you have their willing attention. Information about both is currently easily obtained. Solution-focused therapy involves a client/professional relationship in which questions posed tend to direct the thinking of the client along pragmatic constructive and creative lines. Clients are encouraged to take guilt-free responsibility for themselves and their situations. A question-mark lies over whether they rely more on the commitment and self-belief of the practitioner, and whether what is actually happening is therapy or mentoring.

Rational–emotive therapy

If one considers for a moment four functional domains – that is, behaviour, thinking which controls action, introspective thought, and 'unconscious' processes – then cognitive therapies generally limit themselves to the first two areas, with occasional illuminations of the third.

Rational–emotive therapy (RET) fits broadly into the same cognitive category but penetrates deeper into the third domain of introspective thought. Rational–emotive therapists encourage clients to adopt alternative strategies for thinking, but do so by helping them to re-evaluate their internal worlds, to like themselves better, and to reconcile themselves to life in a way which is less destructive. Its aim is the promotion of fallible but lovable and loving human beings. The objective is to reduce, or eliminate the need for, unrealistic expectations of personal growth.

It may be hard to grasp the difference between cognitive–behavioural approaches and rational–emotive therapy. The secret is in the names. 'Cognitive' gets replaced by 'rational' and 'behavioural' gets replaced by 'emotional'. Cognitive behaviourists do encourage their clients to think about feelings. However, there may be a tendency to treat them as things relative to the more important function of behaviour, and easily manipulated. RET recognises that feelings can sometimes be as firm and unmovable as facts, and the problem often lies in how we think about them.

Clients are encouraged to accept themselves as they are with limitations, and to think about how to make the best of what they do have. Behaviour then changes precisely because clients are no longer trying to be someone or something they are not. Examples of this different kind of thinking are: explaining to people that their depression is a normal reaction to disastrous events, or that they are vulnerable and should not feel ashamed of needing help, and teaching people who get angry that they do not necessarily have to try to stop themselves – they will still get angry, and perhaps for good reason, but that does not mean they should stop focusing on their chosen goals for a high-quality life.

Neurolinguistic programming

Neurolinguistic programming (NLP) veers towards the other side of the cognitive–behavioural framework. Thoughts are seen almost as 'mental behaviour' and thought patterns are seen as learned processes which have an impact on state of mind. The teacher who stands in front of the mirror each morning and says 'I am not going to shout at the children today' is practising neurolinguistic programming. The pupil who stands in front of the mirror each morning and says 'I'm ugly and no-one at school likes me' is also doing so. Such a pupil is more likely to arrive at school depressed and angry and to conflict with staff or peers.

In some cases it may be useful to reprogramme these 'neurolinguistic' patterns. As with behaviour therapy it is probably more effective to do so in an informal way, by reinforcing over and over again the key messages which the pupil will internalise by osmosis. Formal NLP treats the client rather like a subject. The key word in working with difficult children is 'relationships', and NLP does not offer much in direct support of their development.

Role-play, rehearsal and modelling

Strategies like desensitization, flooding, anger management and so on require confidence and clarity of thought as well as the skills to deliver them. As with all the approaches discussed here, school-based professional teams might be able to carry out full-scale programmes themselves, but the alternative is referral to a psychological or psychiatric department. However, the process of desensitisation can also be administered safely and effectively in the context of an enjoyable and approving relationship between teachers, support staff and pupils using role-play, rehearsal and modelling.

These techniques can be amongst the most powerful and yet they are fun. They allow the pupil to rediscover self-control and good humour. At the same time they are a context for learning key lessons for successful school life. Situations the pupil is likely to encounter are rehearsed, and the reactions of the pupil are facilitated in safety. During role-play I once had to 'permanently exclude' a pupil for persistent arguing – this caused great amusement (see Aleem, Appendix 1). However, the serious point was underlined, and the pupil realised that he would have to adopt an alternative strategy which we rehearsed together. It is useful to rehearse the key messages the pupil needs to communicate. It is important that he or she understands the need to assimilate these messages and 'own' them. As school situations are rehearsed and alternative strategies modelled for the pupil and role-played by them, positive messages and concrete rewards reinforce this simple idea: 'This is a good way, and you are a good pupil!'

Mentoring and befriending

The outreach worker, teaching staff and support staff will all act as mentors and befrienders from time to time, when pupils need support and strong direction, exhortation and encouragement. To the degree that a bond of trust and friendship has been forged, within professional boundaries, the pupil will respond positively to this as an aid to 'moving on'.

Mentoring and befriending programmes are a relatively recent phenomenon which have growing popularity, and are often staffed by volunteers. These types of programme may work better when 'attached' to a core resource or institution such as a school. These programmes can extend the work of the school at little or no cost. How much value this would add depends on whether pupil and family want and need such a resource. I have been able to obtain the support of a very effective adult befriender to work with single mothers. In one case this was outstandingly successful, and the pupil's pregnant mother received much needed moral and emotional support which grew into a firm friendship. On another occasion it was less effective, because the mother concerned had too many informal befrienders offering countervailing advice, and an unhealthy preoccupation with a spiritualist 'medium'.

Remedial academic work

There is a debate worth having about the importance of academic deficits, and whether they are, in fact, acting as catalysts for poor and disruptive behaviour. Is the child is being disruptive and distracting, refusing to settle down or getting into fights, solely because he or she cannot do the work? Perhaps, if the academic deficits could be addressed the problems would go away. The danger of this kind of argument is that it supports those who want to simply reinforce the academic resources of the school, and have little time for problem pupils. Children who are very behind are not going to catch up overnight, and they may have learning difficulties that have not been identified or perhaps are not currently recognised as such. Very often the learning deficits are best explained as a result of their other problems, which frequently extend to home life as well.

Consequently, determined remedial action consisting of one-to-one tuition and accelerated learning schemes may be effective. An in-class support teacher may also provide sufficient additional input. These strategies must be supported by a more comprehensive approach. There is no shortage of suitable material and one or two suggestions are made in Appendix 3.

Dealing with non-attendance/truancy/school phobia or anxiety

Although this is grouped here with other strategies for working with the individual, it falls somewhere between individual and family work, involving changes in pupil *and* family as to how they think about the problem, communication and behaviour. Programmes often require modification, because self-exclusion creates a different set of institutional imperatives. But the theoretical underpinning is very similar.

To self-exclude is, strategically, far more effective than to non-attend. Self-excludees are forbidden to attend, whereas non-attenders and truants are coerced to do so. It also creates a second level of meaning, since the presenting issue is obscuring the 'real issue'. If self-exclusion is suspected (for example in Aleem's case, Appendix 1) the first thing to do is to see whether the pupil is able to recognise it. The obvious question is: 'How did you feel once you were excluded?' (answered by expressed relief, happiness, or statements like 'I didn't want to go anyway', or 'teacher wanted me out'). Another is: 'Did you deliberately get yourself thrown out?' Difficulties arise when parental pressure or feelings of guilt oblige the pupil to maintain their earnest wish to be back in school even though their behaviour has told a quite different story.

Programmes for non-attendance, truancy, school phobia or anxiety are numerous and the strategies they incorporate can make a distinct contribution to reintegration. It is the case that such programmes are generally much more successful with younger pupils, and Scott's case (Appendix 1) does illustrate and underline the need to consider what philosophical, as opposed to social, value should be given to the individual wishes of an older pupil who does not wish to return to school. Bridging courses offering older pupils alternatives to school provision (see Appendix 3), with a more grown-up orientation, therefore offer an attractive and important element in the range of provision available to authorities, and of course their clients.

Youth and community programmes

Youth and community programmes, such as car and motorbike projects and arts projects, are usually run by the local Youth Service or voluntary-sector groups. Car and motorbike projects involve young people who might otherwise be getting involved with a delinquent peer group, particularly in stealing vehicles. Small groups of young people meet to dismantle, clean, repair, and occasionally track-ride 'real' bikes. For pupils who are fascinated by engines, this is better than drugs! The slightly anti-establishment figures who run such projects often become mentors by default. Arts and crafts projects can also provide positive and vocational experiences which are stepping stones to more academic curricula for pupils who need motivation and encouragement in a hands-on setting. Local youth clubs can provide a context for social learning and alternatives to street-life.

All these involve liaison with other non-statutory agencies, which can be time-consuming but valuable. However, self-esteem and motivation (and anxiety) are often context- and task-specific and so the benefits of short-term involvements like these may be limited. Such projects might best be viewed as additional resources that the outreach worker can draw upon to complement other initiatives.

Respite breaks

These are not cheap, but a number of organisations exist to help with this or the technicalities of finding a suitable place to go (see Appendix 3). Escort costs are high, and if the pupil is not part of a large group there are no economies of scale. A holiday for pupils should be provided only for clearly thought-out reasons. Criteria can include: redressing chronic underprivilege, educational purposes, parents or carers in need of respite, promotion of peer and group relationships, or opportunities to develop independence.

Simon's is a case in point (see Appendix 1). He went with his favourite support worker (James) and four other pupils for four days to an activity centre, just before returning to school. Simon was an indolent and withdrawn character who had been out of school for too long. The activity centre got him moving again, and the time spent in close quarters with James was an opportunity to encourage him to adopt a more positive approach, and to moan and argue less. He confessed to being anxious about school and very negative about the future. James helped him to talk through his concerns 'around the camp-fire' and his reintegration was a success. In Aleem's case valuable lessons about independence and growing up appear to have been learned in similar circumstances.

It is not always easy to see how such an event changes behaviour. However, for most of us childhood holidays are an enduring and important memory of life-affirming events. Raymond, who had barely been out of London throughout his life, spent 10 days beside (and indeed on) a Scottish Loch in serene surroundings, with a loving and sympathetic family. If this experience has been internalised at all (and why would it not be?) then its beneficial effect may work through in crucial ways that are, quite reasonably, very difficult to identify.

Respite break opportunities could be provided as rewards for achievement, and in a few cases this might be appropriate – if the pupil is keen. However, if the child is very discouraged or depressed, the risk of failure could make such an approach risky.

▓▓▓▓ Working with families and pupils

Family group conferences (FGCs)

Family group conferences are potentially the single most effective way of involving families and schools in cases where a pupil is at serious risk of school failure. The Family Rights Group can provide training and advice (see Appendix 3)

This way of working with children and families originated in New Zealand as a response to the high numbers of Maori children involved with social services. It was recognised that extensive family and clan relationships which could respond to the needs of the child were being ignored, and so an approach that could tap the family group's potential for arriving at an effective care plan was devised.

At a case conference, the professionals make a plan which the family have to accept; at a family group conference it is the other way round (although the concerns are the same in each case).

This change of emphasis is reflected in the way people are invited, how the conference is structured, and the management of the outcome. When an FGC works, it is because the family have come up with solutions they can then own. It is an empowering technique that will probably fail if the family do not wish to be empowered. Most do, but some do not. Another weak point is that professionals are sometimes reluctant to accept the family's role and may undermine or sabotage the plan.

There are several stages to the process:

1. The co-ordinator (an independent person, or the outreach worker, or other programme personnel) invites to a conference all involved family members, and facilitates their attendance (family in this case means all members of the family's personal network).

2. At the conference, professionals involved with the family present their concerns. When inviting the professionals they are asked to ensure their report is family-friendly – avoiding jargon, peremptory judgments, or over-detailed chronologies. The co-ordinator ensures that the family have an opportunity to ask for clarification.

3. After summarising these concerns as a limited number of action points, the co-ordinator and other professionals leave the family to discuss them, and arrive at a plan. The co-ordinator may have to tactfully pop in and help them stay on track and purposeful, but must avoid getting drawn into acting as an arbiter or judge.

4. Finally, the co-ordinator helps the family to draft the plan on paper, and present it to concerned professionals.

Many social services are adopting this model, and so frequently a social worker will need to approve the plan. Unless there are child-protection issues outstanding there is an expectation that they will do so. However, if the approach is used as an in-house strategy, there are no other professional agencies who need to accept the plan.

The model is amenable to creative modification. The independence of the co-ordinator is a key factor in its success, and whilst the outreach worker may be a sufficiently 'independent' figure, it might be quite useful if colleagues coordinated each other's FGCs.

Counselling and counselling skills

Counselling is a generic term which is often preceded by a qualifier such as 'bereavement' or 'careers'. As this approach proliferates so do its detractors, who complain in words to the effect that 'there is too much of it'. One might also say there is also too little of it since, as a process, it is almost impossible to audit and all too easily deteriorates into advice-giving, or even conversation. The Audit Commission (1995) described 'general counselling' as 'particularly ineffective' in preventing re-offending. However, many of the 'promising targets' identified in the report – such as changing antisocial attitudes and feelings, promoting family affection, communication, supervision and monitoring, and increased self-control, self-management and problem-solving skills – could be amenable to careful counselling and mentoring intervention.

Counselling is generally seen as a non-directive process. However, in the case of young people it is sometimes more valuable to provide some focus for the sessions, and input ideas which the pupil can take on board and work into a form that is recognisable to themselves. As the degree of directedness increases, the process of counselling becomes more recognisable as 'mentoring'. If it focuses on core skills it becomes 'coaching'.

A distinction can be made between 'counselling' as a therapeutic method (which carries the specific label, and has boundaries of time, place and duration) and 'counselling skills' which can be viewed as a technique (or group of techniques) applicable to numerous situations. Counselling skills can extend the effectiveness of anyone engaged in a client/professional relationship, complementing and enhancing the application of many other strategies including teaching. Their informal use in a variety of settings works well with children, particularly younger children, whereas parents may prefer to be involved in a more clearly defined formal process. However, when meetings take place for the sole purpose of engaging in a counselling relationship, the explicit commitment of the client to such a relationship is a prerequisite. The choice of setting is open, so long as boundaries are maintained. Ground rules may vary provided they are mutually agreed, and do not compromise child protection.

Counselling skills can be thought of as requiring two components: those of active listening and of understanding people. Active listening is a wonderful skill that everybody should learn; it also develops interpersonal and intrapersonal awareness. Understanding people grows out of 'taught psychology', and 'psychology' derived from experience, together with context-specific understandings, such as 'family dynamics'. Counselling skills are generally taught as part of a process through learning, role-play, disclosure, and group work.

Counselling was used as one strategy in the cases of John (see Appendix 1) and of another boy, Charles. In both cases there was an initial reluctance to engage with a process about which the pupils knew nothing. Adults often have experience of being 'clients' and slip naturally into the role, which assists a rapid transition to the middle stage of the counselling process. Furthermore, both pupils had characteristic difficulties expressing themselves. To overcome this, John used poetry and Charles used drawing. In other cases, the task of providing counselling was delegated to a specialist with experience of working with young black men.

In John's case, one session was devoted to convincing him that he had problems that needed addressing, despite his assertions to the contrary, by the simple expedient of showing him that everyone had problems. Another session was devoted to helping him see the links between how he felt and how he acted. A breakthrough came when he was given a writing assignment to describe these links. He proved to have quite a poetic literary ability.

Cognitive interviewing

Interviewing in the wider sense of the word is something the outreach worker does regularly, either as part of the process of understanding the pupil's thinking (or the parent's), or in order to help in gaining a more comprehensive picture of the circumstances leading up to exclusion or some other life-event.

Cognitive interviewing developed from research into memory function; it has been taken up by the police force as a means of enhancing the ability of witnesses to recall essential details, and to challenge the veracity of suspect's evidence. Whilst there is no suggestion that the outreach worker should indulge in 'police work', a process of detection may sometimes be necessary to help the pupil and the outreach worker gain insights. Cognitive interviewing is an effective and generally pleasant technique which (as with counselling skills) can be used either formally or in a natural setting.

The cognitive interviewer adopts the role of facilitator and garners understanding in a flexible and non-directive way. For instance, information is disclosed in a spontaneous sequence following the internal processes of the interviewee, and so not necessarily in a logical order. But in addition the interviewer can help the interviewee to build up a more dynamic and comprehensive picture by asking follow-up questions that depend on a careful attention to detail and an ability to enter into the scenario described without prejudice and with an open mind. Positive attitude, sensitivity and awareness will improve the chances of memory recovery.

Good rapport is an important precursor, followed by setting clear ground-rules, recreating the physical and social context, and encouraging 'free reporting', after which the follow-up questions can fill in the details. Another useful technique is to work backwards in time so that more recent events are linked to those just before, and so on. Generally this will work better where the interviewer already has the 'forward' picture and can prompt the interviewee from time to time from notes. The technique rests on careful and detailed research into memory function, and it would be worth reading up the technique fully before trying to apply it, even though many aspects seem familiar from other settings (for further information see Appendix 3).

Art, music, family and similar therapies

Occasionally, a pupil or family may benefit from a structured prescriptive therapy. Art and music therapy are useful ways of helping a pupil to express inner feelings which may have become trapped. One difficulty, which is discussed in more detail in Chapter 9, is that ordinary cases of difficulty at school are not seen as serious enough to warrant substantial resources. The pupil and the family may not be willing to invest the time and commitment required. However, social services do have funds they can allocate for therapy, and if their co-operation has been gained they can open a file on a family and leave it as allocated to the duty-worker (effectively unallocated). They can then refer the pupil to a therapist or other service as required.

A similar approach can be used to obtain healthcare services, by persuading the family to visit the local GP, possibly with a covering letter. The GP can then refer the family directly to various primary care services.

▓▓ Supporting parents and 'therapy by proxy'

There is considerable evidence that personal stress influences functioning in the workplace. For instance, emotional/personal problems and stress have been identified as the second main cause of absence from work (Balcombe *et al.*, 1993), and poor parenting or family conflict is related to delinquency and underachievement (Loeber and Dishion, 1984; Snyder and Patterson, 1987). One way to reduce stress levels for schoolchildren is to reduce stress levels in their carer.

In Shane's case (see Appendix 1), reducing parental anxiety and providing an outlet for her concerns about the future (through regular counselling sessions and the involvement of a volunteer befriender) reduced the pressure on Shane. Once he had started back at school, his mother became very anxious about academic standards and an incident of bullying. Her urge to take him out of school was restrained by more-or-less daily exhortations not to do so until he had had time to prove himself, although she was also assured that she would be supported in any decisions she made for Shane.

In other cases, carers would have benefited from more support but rejected it, or were already involved with other agencies. Allocating significant resources to the parents is justified where the pupil is clearly under pressure from them and where that pressure constitutes a specific and substantial element in their problems in school.

Work with parents usually takes a more informal line, with the focus on facilitating disclosure. The hardest thing for parents to do is tell someone in authority that they feel guilty about their own shortcomings. It is on a basis of trust and mutual respect that parents are able to talk about what they know is really wrong, and to hear what they can do to effect a change.

▓▓ Social services and healthcare services involvement

From time to time the needs of a pupil or their family require the input of other specialties: an obvious example was Aleem's need for a speech therapist (see Appendix 1). Most social services departments will have a family service unit or equivalent which exists to support families that are struggling, by providing grants, practical help and advice.

It is important when involving other agencies to recognise that to do so is to bring into play another agency culture – with all that that may imply for the family and pupil concerned in terms of form-filling, questions and answers, involvements, and possible advice or expectations which may run counter to the outreach worker's.

Where there is the likelihood that children may be at risk of significant harm, social services need to be informed. At the very first meeting, almost before anything else is said, the outreach worker should have made this sort of statement to both pupil and family (see also Appendix 2):

> *I will keep everything you say strictly in confidence, and just between you and me. But if you tell me something which makes me think a child might be at risk of harm, I will talk to you about my concerns and we can decide together who we need to tell.*

The statement would be modified for different ages and abilities – it may be necessary to explain the word 'confidential'. Such a statement subtly makes it clear that secrets will be kept, but safety will be paramount, and in any case nothing will be done without first talking to the people concerned. It is a curious fact that this statement, made at the first meeting, has never created ill-will. If made at any later time, it will seem as if you are responding to existing concerns, and suspicions and hackles will be raised.

It should not need saying – but for safety's sake must be – that if a professional thinks there may be a child at risk no attempt should be made to question those concerned, or gather evidence. It is all too easy to taint any subsequent police or social services enquiry. There may be an assumption that behind every child who is difficult at school there is a family-at-risk. This is not the case.

8 The special problem of reintegrating permanently excluded children

▦ The nature of the problem

The status of permanently excluded children is uncertain. In the majority of cases, whether the pupil is now assigned home tuition, or enrolled in a Pupil Referral Unit (PRU) or other education centre, or offered a place at a special school, *the focus should be on returning to a mainstream school*. A tiny proportion of younger pupils may need special environments – which I take to mean institutions other than schools for children with emotional and behavioural difficulties (EBD) – where a multiprofessional team of psychologists, psychiatrists, social and healthcare workers, and teachers provide real therapy in a community setting. Many older children are much happier with the kind of vocational/work-experience provision in a college environment which is increasingly being made available.

There would be a risk of repetition if detailed planning frameworks were set down here. Much of what has already been said about reintegrating children at risk of school failure applies also to the permanently excluded returnee. The same principles apply, and similar kinds of intervention are needed, embedded in the same kind of inside perspective. The case studies in Appendix 1 give a number of real-life examples of how the process can work. The flow diagrams in this chapter suggest the procedural pathway, and the accompanying text explains the context. However, there is a significant difference between children at risk of school failure and permanently excluded returnees – in the former case intervention and reintegration into the heart of the school takes place within one school, but in the latter case two schools are involved, together with another agency or an outreach worker in between. Towards the end of the chapter the questions of who does what and when are considered.

Permanently excluded children frequently have long histories of difficulty in school, and the conclusion follows that the problem is chronic and obscure, caused by some unknown historical cause. However, the needs of the pupil may never have been addressed, and as time passes the increasing educational deficit – and hence the aversion to school (and feelings that the teachers 'don't care', and 'aren't helping') – is actually extending the severity of a problem that has a solution, hidden from the school but not necessarily invisible to the outreach worker.

If the strategy of reintegrating pupils with SEN Statements were ever sanctioned, a significant proportion of these children, and those currently at EBD schools, could be reintegrated successfully, although pupils who had been at an EBD school for some time would require a slightly different strategy.

Only 15–20 per cent of permanently excluded secondary-aged pupils return to the mainstream, and only 27 per cent of primary-aged children (Parsons, 1995, 1999). Since one may assume that the older pupils were more likely to be classed as 'dropped out', this suggests that about 70 per cent of Key Stage 2 and 3 exclusions are provided for on a continuing basis by education otherwise or by special provision, with costs accruing annually until the pupil reaches school leaving age. A pupil starting at Year 7 sent to an EBD school will cost at least £60,000 over the following five years. A Year 8 pupil referred to a PRU will cost £5000–8000 a year for however long he or she remains there. In other words, if a reintegration programme costing under £5000 is tried for all pupils currently in Year 7 at EBD schools, and the programme is successful for only 20 per cent of them, it will more than pay for itself. Such a low threshold for success argues in favour of developing this initiative wherever possible.

One study (Grizenko et al., 1994) found that children who were younger, with better reading skills, no ADHD (attention deficit hyperactivity disorder), and who experienced little parental discord were more likely to be successfully reintegrated into 'regular' school. The DfEE sees a difference in outlook for younger and older children. The younger the excluded pupil the more powerful is the argument for expediting a return to a mainstream setting, and plans should reflect this clearly. Older children, on the other hand, are more resistant to a return to the school culture, but may well be motivated by opportunities in vocational learning with a 'world of work' orientation, and some access to National Curriculum subjects.

DfEE advice to schools on permanent exclusion is that there should be a very clear learning plan, with objectives and targets, and time scales for achievement. An excellent example is given of one authority that declares: 'supported schools see the reintegration of excluded pupils as part of their role' and 'reintegration starts at the point of exclusion' (DfEE, 1999 – case study on p. 38). The importance is stressed of having a named worker managing the provision. The DfEE's stance is, however, wholly impracticable in suggesting that excluded pupils should start at a new mainstream school 'within days or weeks'. Weeks perhaps, but any return to school should coincide with the start of a new term (or if necessary half-term).

The advice that 'the longer a young person is out of school the more difficult it can be for them to reintegrate' (DfEE, 1999 – para. 7.1) is also slightly off-centre. Whilst older children may drift further out of the school culture, younger ones may benefit from a period of 'seclusion' provided that something effective is happening for them in terms of intervention. Those who want to return to school become more and more motivated to do so as the loneliness sets in, and (speaking brutally) the threshold criteria can be raised in stages by the outreach worker who gatekeeps access to a new school, so that the pupil is challenged to perform new feats of effort and commitment in trying to reach reading targets, homework targets, or agreeing to role-play new behaviours, and promising to 'follow through' once they are enrolled.

■ Phases of reintegration

The process of reintegration has four phases characterised as 'picking up the pieces', 'walking together', 'swimming upriver' and 'just don't look back' (see Figure 18). Phase one is called 'picking up the pieces' because, in addition to the fragmentation and disintegration which led to permanent exclusion, there is a sense of failure and additional rejection and a fear of further rejection in the future. A period of supported progress is usually essential. Rejected children are often pathetically grateful for someone who shows real interest in their progress and are ready to re-invent themselves if they are shown how.

Getting back into a school really is a movement against the flow. Most children find it hard enough to cope with a new school at the start of Year 7 when all the other children also are new and special induction programmes are in place. It is that much harder for returnees, who may find themselves re-enacting history. Successful children are the ones who 'don't look back'.

It is essential to promote a proactive approach from senior managers, exemplified by the head teacher, whilst the transfer of power and authority from the outreach worker to the school is taking place. There is great significance in the DfEE's statement that 'supported schools see the reintegration of excluded pupils as part of their role'. Many schools, and many teachers, see exclusion as a political issue, and the return of excluded children as an establishment attempt to 'offload' the problem on to them. This is so misguided and a sad reflection on the sense of alienation which such teachers feel in themselves. They have lost sight of the pupils' humanity and in the process are distorting their own.

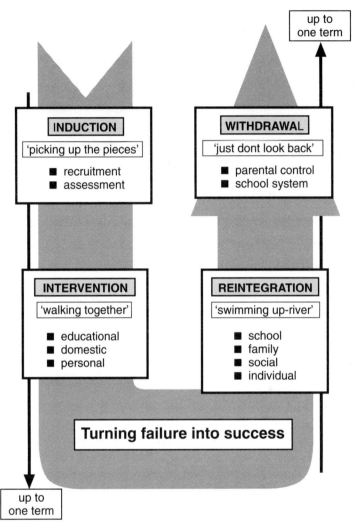

Figure 18

When staff are opposed to a pupil's inclusion, pastoral support will not be forthcoming, pupil–staff relationships will be slow to form, and the pupil will be covertly isolated.

Picking up the pieces

Once a pupil is permanently excluded, a secondary raft of problems are grafted on to the comprehensively confused and dis-enabling outlook of a pupil previously only at-risk of school failure through exclusion. Additional and discouraging elements in the equation are:

- much more guilt and more anger in both pupil and family;
- a drastic reduction in educational input, leading to increasing academic deficits;
- a breakdown in healthy lifestyle habits such as getting up in time for school, no PE or sports, loss of stimulating and competitive public environment, and so on;
- increased anxiety about the future, especially panic over finding a school;
- increased risk of, and opportunities for, delinquent behaviour;
- increased pressure on domestic circumstances and family life.

These factors need to be acknowledged and addressed within the process of reintegration.

It is some consolation that the healing effects of time and the natural process of maturation will now work together and make the task of developing the pupil's perspective easier, which can be expedited by an empathic no-blame approach from the outreach worker who encourages the growth of self-respect and hope in the future. A core objective is always to enable a pupil to accept responsibility for his or her situation. It is unusual to find a pupil who will not acknowledge the value of 'education', although regrettably the same cannot always be said for 'school'. Facing up to the fear of failure, and awareness of educational shortcomings, is never easy; but where the main problem is self-confidence, or academic weakness is subject-specific, one-to-one tuition can achieve a great deal – although the educational part of the programme is no substitute for a school curriculum in the long term. A period of success, forged between the unhappy past and the uncertain future, acts as a shield and a starting block.

Time elapsed between applying for a school place and obtaining a start date can be excessive, sometimes more than a term. A lot will depend on who is managaing the reintegration – where there is little out-of-school support, the pupil may have too many opportunities to develop out-of-school associations (such as street-life). Children are sometimes turned down on spurious grounds; and although these decisions would probably have been overturned on appeal, to do so would also generate considerable hostility. Incoming pupils should be linked into the SEN department as a stage 2 (SENCoP) referral.

� Walking together

Outreach workers have to be prepared for a broad range of demands on their expertise and have some sense of when it is appropriate to take responsibility, and when it is necessary to seek advice or refer to other agencies. The range of strategies available will depend primarily on the skills base of the outreach worker, but also on possible collaborative support from colleagues.

Once again, a metaphor is used to capture the concreteness of the task. The objective of the planning process is to create a 'pathway'. 'Plans' can

4th week

From platform to pathway ....

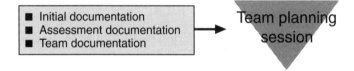

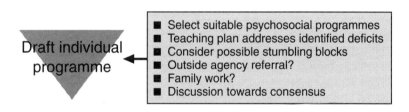

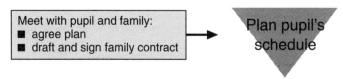

Figure 19

be technical, often highly detailed, and may be written using code, symbols and diagrams, with a distinct lack of plain English. Pathways are easy to follow, guide the walker safely across unknown country, and you may not even need a map (see Figure 19).

The strategic framework provided by the individual plan needs to be backed up by an action plan identifying specific objectives, and the resources required to achieve them. This action plan needs to be modest and practical, because there are only limited time and resources available to achieve the required goal. The outreach worker is not there to transform the pupil's whole life – just to get him or her ready to risk the leap back into education and set the person up to develop the skills and receive the necessary support to sustain it. This leap is metaphorically into cold water, and the course is upstream.

There is the question of visiting the previous school to talk with staff about their experiences. The difficulty here is that their image has become fixed by the process of exclusion. Time has already passed and, psychologically speaking, the insightful material may have been jettisoned. Teachers are busy with their current problems, and there is nothing on-going to tap into which relates to the pupil. Sometimes verbal reports from sympathetic teachers are at variance with the formal reports on file. Often there are one or two teachers who want to share their sense of concern about the pupil's welfare, or relate more positive aspects of their time in school. It is well worth having this information.

▓ Swimming up-river

In educational terms, the process of reintegration needs to be comparatively quick (see Figure 20). At the earliest half-termly start possible the process of review is overtaken by the involvement of a receiving school, who will review progress themselves. Staff are often suspicious of excluded pupils and this is understandable, though a little unprofessional.

The art and science of public relations is to help others to think what you want them to think, by fair means not foul. Generally, this has to be done against a prevailing tide of opinion or belief. The general message that the outreach worker must get across is this: *Excluded pupils are not monsters, they need help to heal, and punishment is inappropriate.* The specific message is:

- This pupil has had *these* problems and we have done *this* to remedy them.

- The pupil and family have done what is required of them and we have every confidence that the pupil will succeed at this new school, because it has *these* qualities that our pupil needs.

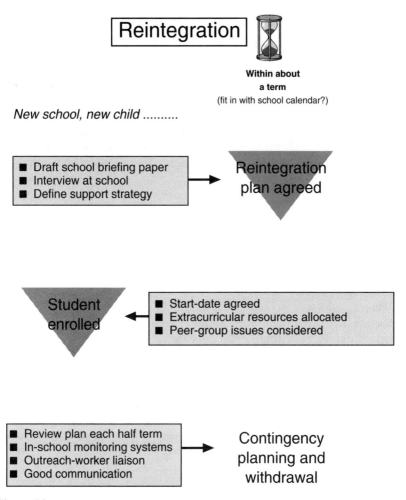

Figure 20

- An outreach worker will deliver *the following levels of support* initially and can offer *the following strategies* to ensure a successful return to school.

A briefing paper written by the new head teacher (with help from the outreach worker) is a useful way to enable staff to understand the circumstances and needs of the returnee. Writing this is a delicate task.

- There needs to be information, but there also needs to be a respecting of confidentiality.

- There needs to be detail, but not too much.

- The objective is to inform sufficiently, and to elicit sympathy.

Staff should not see the document as an early warning of likely problems, which in the worst cases become self-fulfilling prophecies. A skilled head teacher will ensure that the message on the grapevine is simple and solution-focused: 'He or she is coping with *this* stressor, and is not so bad, responding well to *this* approach.'

The support strategy, especially at the beginning, needs to be very clear. It may involve parents or other family members, but it is managed and 'owned' by the school. The plan should consider the peer group issues – will the pupil need help to make friends, is there likely to be pressure from a clique in the school, or even a need to have 'sparring contests' to establish the pecking order. It is possible that the returning pupil will get drawn towards other disaffected pupils. Sometimes it is as if the pupil has to go through the process of working out boundaries and reliving conflicts all over again. The objective is to intermediate so that the outcomes are different.

This is why the school's commitment to an inclusive ethos is so important. A returning pupil should have fewer problems, but in a proportion of cases there will be relapses into bad behaviour, and possibly a crisis. This time the outreach worker and parents are there, fully aware of issues in and out of school, and able to provide a quick response to problems. Senior managers will need to remind staff (possibly again and again) that the pupil is not expected to be perfect, but only to remain within the broad parameters of the school's behavioural standards. A good question is: '*How would we respond to the same behaviour from Matthew?*', who is well known to staff and reasonably well liked in the school.

'Threshold criteria' are targets, agreed between all parties, that a pupil must achieve to earn the right to go into a new school. The use of threshold criteria may not always be appropriate, where goals and interventions are difficult to quantify. They are a psychological sleight-of-hand, useful for convincing pupils who lack confidence that they are ready for the big leap, and to show staff who may be anxious that the pupil can show a record of recent achievement and stick to contracts. Examples of threshold criteria might be minimum session attendance rate, specific targets on a learning programme achieved, a letter of apology written and sent to a pupil hurt by the excluded pupil, and so on. Threshold criteria need to be very carefully considered. If they do not work they can become a barrier to progress, or just another example of boundaries that move. One or two criteria should be sufficient, or do not use them at all.

Letting go (withdrawal)

The reintegration plan needs to consider what individual education plan the staff should deliver, how long support teachers who have been working with the pupil prior to enrolment should continue to do so in school, and what the family needs to do to support the process. There needs to be a named worker (teaching or non-teaching staff) who can provide moral, emotional and practical support indefinitely and as needed. Social and individual concerns need to be addressed, and the primary objectives are to enable the in-school staff to manage the pupil (with the family's help), and to enable the pupil to hold down a school place. However, there also needs to be a contingency plan that covers the possibility of recidivism (see Figure 21).

It may be that the outreach worker needs to remain closely involved during the first few weeks, and less frequently for up to a term. The SEN

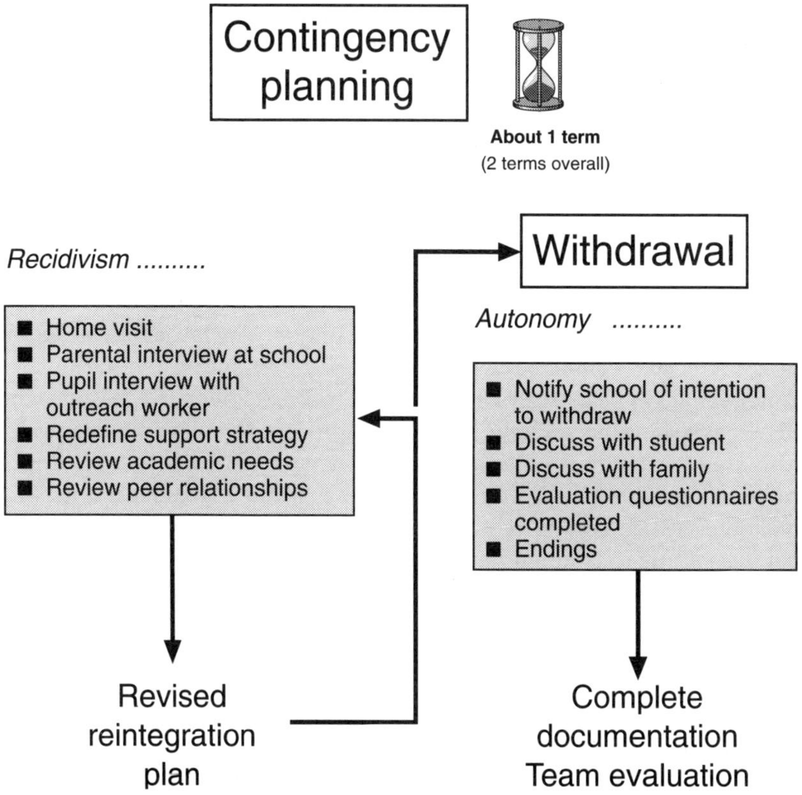

Figure 21

department will provide the pupil with on-going support. But the pupil should be able to function independently from an early stage. The outreach worker is not there to prop up a weak pupil but to give a boosted start to a prodigal one. It is not in principle wrong for the outreach worker to continue as the named worker after reintegration is complete, but it may be impracticable since the specialist skills of the outreach worker will be needed elsewhere.

It is important that all members of staff directly involved with the pupil, led by the head or senior manager, should take the initiative in managing the pupil's induction. Where there is reluctance to admit the pupil, or high anxiety about how the reintegration will work out, teachers can sometimes employ an isolationist strategy, as if the pupil were (metaphorically) in quarantine. The responsibility for in-school support and liaison then seems to remain with the outreach worker and normal school rules do not appear to apply. The pupil can feel marginalised and does not learn to follow the overt or covert rules of the new school.

Someone from within the school must take pastoral responsibility for the pupil's wellbeing, including handing out sanctions where necessary. The outreach worker must allow the named worker to plan the reintegration (with tactful and diplomatically delivered advice). Once staff have made a plan, they have an investment in its success.

Who does what, and when

There is an old joke about a tourist who stopped his car in a quiet country lane and asked a farmer for directions to London. The farmer scratched his head and said: 'Ooh-arrr, well if I was going to London I wouldn't start from here at all.' A similar sort of answer could be given to a head teacher who was asking about how to set up a process for managing returning permanent excludees. Another analogy might be to ask: if a ship is foundering at sea, should onlookers start to build a lifeboat if one is not available? All choices have shortcomings in such a situation: one cannot just do nothing and watch the sailors drown, but building a lifeboat is too complicated and would take too long, and swimming out with lifebelts is likely to put others at risk. Luckily the analogy is not exact; or to stretch it further, there are bits of lifeboat floating about in the water, and someone with the right skills can probably assemble them in time.

These 'bits of lifeboat' are in fact the locally available support assessment and intervention services within and without the school. Within the school, personnel who can take on the role of outreach worker may be members of the SEN department, support teachers, home–school liaison workers, community and ethnic minority workers, or senior teachers with pastoral responsibility. Outreach work could be carried out by different people from time to time, or by a special appointee. Outside the school there may be an effective PRU, or a specialist unit within EWS, EPS, the Youth Service, or possibly even a social services department. The local authority may have its own initiative, and voluntary agencies may be working in the area.

In the DfEE case study (DfEE, 1999), a local PRU provides this service. Outreach workers are school-based for part of the time, and also in the PRU. The local education authority names the school to be attended. A pupil is reintegrated as soon as the threshold criteria are reached, and the named school then takes on the responsibility for managing reintegration supported by the PRU with parents fully involved. This arrangement meets the infrastructural requirements well. It is not a criticism to say that the successful development and continuing effectiveness of this facility is dependent on the personnel who run it, the management skills of the LEA, and the professionalism of senior managers in the participating schools. These elements will not be found in every locality. However, every school will have a department for special educational needs, and as a minimum standard SEN and non-teaching staff must be encouraged, trained and supported to do this work. There needs to be overlap between local schools.

Consider the four key tasks again: (1) picking up the pieces; (2) walking together; (3) swimming up-river; and (4) letting go. The first two stages are out-of-school, and the last two are in-school. But for the sake of continuity all four stages must be co-ordinated by the same person.

- If the outreach worker is school-based, then the receiving school must be chosen at stage 1.

- If the outreach worker is based partly in school and partly elsewhere, then the receiving school can be chosen at any time up to the beginning of stage 3, the point of return to school.

- If the outreach worker is wholly based off-site then the receiving school can be chosen at any time before stage 3, but there is a special problem here. The outreach worker will come into the school as an outsider, and this can create serious difficulties. There are two kinds of problem: difficulties persuading schools to be involved in reintegration (see below), and resistance by staff towards external personnel arriving with a problem and passing the pupil over, with good advice.

Who chooses the receiving school? In law, parents do have some rights in this area, and schools are not allowed to refuse a pupil a place solely because he or she has been permanently excluded. In practice, this has happened in the past. There is something to be said for managing all admissions centrally, and relieving the head teacher from making a difficult and perhaps controversial decision. However, inclusive schools will want to reintegrate pupils wherever possible: outreach workers should definitely not be based wholly outside the school, unless the local education authority handles admissions centrally and will assign a pupil to the receiving school. Otherwise the outreach worker will spend a disproportionate amount of time trying to find a school that will accept the pupil.

Actually, every school will need outreach workers to help prevent exclusions, and it may well make sense for the same personnel to handle incoming pupils. At the same time, the LEA must make provision for the pupil whilst the child is out of school (in this model, stages 1 and 2); but continuity across the four stages is essential. There is a key issue here: schools, off-site education centres and the LEA must work together in an integrated way. If the provision for permanently excluded pupils is isolated from the mainstream the task of reintegration will be made much more difficult. The exact make-up of the integrated service could be LEA-controlled, a strategy of managed moves from school to school, through local agreement, or managed by the EWS or EPS, or voluntary agency, or a PRU-centred approach. But the education service, as a whole, must establish a continuity of provision across the four stages, none of which can be avoided.

It must also be recognised that practice in many areas is wholly at variance with principle. Excluded pupils are still spending a year or more with virtually no education other than home tuition whilst a place is sought, and many local education authorities have no-one who can direct and develop a strategic approach. Schools should therefore consider what they can do themselves, *starting with prevention of exclusion.*

There is Standards Funding available, particularly up to the year 2001, which schools can apply for (with the LEA). This should be seen as an opportunity to increase the quality of services that schools can provide, through setting up in-school projects to reduce the strain on teachers and tension in class, by addressing the needs of children at risk of school failure.

A salutary story

Nahim was a refugee, originally from Ethiopia, who had travelled via Turkey, Thailand and Germany to the UK. He had been to primary school in Ethiopia, and then travelled for six years, sometimes with his parents and sometimes with brothers or other relatives. He spoke reasonable but limited English by the time I met him, but could hardly read or write (he could only barely write in Arabic). He had been placed in a mainstream school in Year 8 and expected to sink or swim with the other pupils. It is not clear how the authorities expected him to cope.

Nahim had experienced too much in his childhood that was destructive and damaging. He had watched people being shot in Tigrani, seen family members being tortured, and been separated from his mother at a tender age, and this culminated in him being placed in an environment which he did not understand and which, for all he knew, was as transitory as all the others. Not unusually, he had learned quickly the superficial lessons (which trainers, which shirt, where to go for entertainment, what music to listen to, which television programmes were 'cool', and so on). It was as if everything worth having costed money. He could not cope with the work, and took to petty crime and extortion as ways to express himself and to obtain the money he felt he needed for day-to-day life.

After a very long and substantial intervention involving a saturation literacy programme, cultural awareness, a period in a private school for children who had English as an additional language, art therapy, respite breaks with a family in an Essex farmhouse, and a visit to Brighton, we began the process of enrolling him in a school where several of his relatives were pupils. Unfortunately, his record travelled before him, and one particular teacher was very resistant to his reintegration. The problem was that this teacher was also head-of-upper-school. His guerilla resistance campaign would have been amusing if it had not had such a damaging effect on Nahim.

Firstly, it took nearly four months to get him admitted. One of the difficulties when applying to schools is that you cannot do so lightly. For instance, schools are likely to ignore written requests to place an excluded pupil, or simply write back and say no. In practice, the number of schools in the locality that have places may be small. It is not possible to make a strong and determined attempt to have a pupil enrolled at more than one school at a time. So if a school is being difficult but does not have legal grounds for refusal, one is obliged to keep up the pressure, even though a reluctant school may simply re-exclude. In the case in question, the reluctance was on the part of this one teacher.

After enrolment, Nahim was not allowed to join classes full-time, but had to have one-to-one tuition on-site. The head-of-year refused to acknowledge his existence, and was never heard to address him directly. His antipathy extended to the support workers who were also rudely ignored, and were unable to obtain information on which class Nahim was in. They were never given a timetable. After one term I discovered he was not on the school's computer register. The school also refused to carry out any sanctions, and when Nahim broke any rules we were expected to punish him. Nahim was learning a curious and distorted view of the school culture, and was being kept in ignorance as much as possible.

By great good fortune this teacher left at the end of term, and immediately everything changed. Nahim found out who his tutor was for the first time! A meeting was arranged at which a transfer of authority took place. Nahim was given a tutor group, and his proper integration began.

In the dark days of rejection following exclusion, the only lifeline for the pupil and the family is the reintegration programme. As gatekeeper to a new school, the outreach worker can act with great authority – using this fact as a powerful lever. But pupils become attached to their school, accept new figures in authority, learn the rules (written and unwritten), and form alliances with their peers. The outreach worker is then redundant, and happily so.

The following message is one of the many that outreach workers need to convey to their colleagues:

> *This returning pupil is not going to be an angel, but his behaviour should be within the bounds of what you expect from all your other pupils. Just treat him the way you treat all the others – that's all we ask.*

9 Conclusion

Views on the problem of children at risk of school failure are many and fragmented. One thing is clear – this should be seen as a special educational needs (SEN) issue, not bad behaviour. Recent figures show that the worst boroughs exclude about nine times as many children as the best boroughs (see Appendix 2). Exclusion is not the only option and in many countries it is unheard of, so there is a compelling argument for developing integrated and inclusive approaches. Jacob's story told at the beginning of this book is by no means unique, and shows how easy it still is for children with special needs to slip through the net.

Teachers who recognise the relational aspects of their role are likely to handle difficult children more effectively, because they know that it is not only the children who need to change. Everyone involved makes a contribution to the numerous relationships which develop within a group or class, and to their success or failure. Schools are there to serve the community, and cannot pick and choose pupils, any more than firemen can choose their blazes. The cycle of antisocial behaviour and social alienation runs through the school culture from generation to generation and it can be redirected by alterations in the mindset of decision-makers. Everyone involved needs to take their share of responsibility for a pupil's failure.

Schools can overcome disadvantageous social conditions by creating a positive ethos. Someone has to take responsibility for managing the interventions that pupils in difficulty need. Children often react emotionally to problems and are very changeable, and this can also be true of parents. Both will respond better to professionals who have an inclusive style and an egalitarian approach. Affection should not be thought of as out of place in an educational setting, or indeed within 'social work'. Professionals should have internalised a sense of appropriate boundaries and have the confidence to be responsive and empathic. The specific interventions used will depend on the unique circumstances of the case, and although these strategies are often about producing 'soft change' (i.e. in attitudes, feelings, relationships, awareness and understanding) they need to be well-structured.

Mainstream education provides the most ideal culture for developing children, and is a more likely context within which to break the cycle of failure. It is also the cheapest form of education.

Just as there are wide variations between local authorities and between schools, there are also disquieting differences between children from different ethnic and cultural backgrounds. The data suggest that the processes are inconsistently managed and controlled, and therefore wide open to abuse and unfairness. The benefits of a programme which tackles school failure and its underlying causes benefit society as a whole, but resourcing such programmes falls on the education budget. It is inherently difficult to produce the kind of 'evidence' of success that sceptics and political opponents demand, although people directly involved can clearly see the benefits.

The psychological and emotional damage caused by exclusion should not be underestimated. The wounded soldier leans heavily on a crutch, and the crutch breaks (soldier is to pupil, as crutch is to ?). Children on the margins or beyond the margins need our help to return to the school, as well as constant encouragement and support to help them overcome their own failings. In too many cases, they are also trying to overcome the failings of individual professionals who lack competence or insight! There is a clear need for improved professional development here.

Should we reconsider our expectations? Does child X deserve Y hours of extra support and encouragement, and Z degrees of special consideration before the case is given up as lost? Or does child X deserve everything that it is within the school's power to provide? Senior managers who take the latter view will exclude far fewer children, or even none. It must be remembered that the vast majority of exclusions are for persistent minor offending. For instance, only 12 exclusions in a 1000 are related to physical violence to teachers. A simple four-point plan will meet the needs of all pupils: improve communications, share perspectives fairly, and rebuild damaged relationships at home and at school. The challenge lies in achieving these simple objectives.

Pupils may use the exclusion process to escape the demands of school life. Fear of failure, of adulthood and of GCSEs may be confused with domestic difficulties. Though it is not the schools' fault, we do have a responsibility to try to reverse the situation. This is partly a training issue. The process of 'self-exclusion' goes unrecognised by schools (who do not have access to the motivational processes in a pupil's mind) and by the pupils themselves, since they are 'in denial'. The sense of grievance and loss felt by excluded pupils is paralleled by that of the parents. The importance of 'loss' in development is little understood and may be exacerbated by (or even account for) social–relational disability. Our understanding of complex psychosocial problems is still rudimentary, and education managers may often find themselves excluding someone who merits treatment rather than punishment.

Pupils in difficulties have problems that can be described as school phobic, emotionally disturbed, or delinquent, but it is the meaning behind the behaviour which we need to address.

Pupils who have learning difficulties may not have behavioural problems as well, although this can be a large part of the problem particularly where there are self-esteem issues. Behavioural difficulties are a form of social disability, and the education system has a moral duty to address these as an institutional as well as an individual problem. It is possible that some psychological disorders need redefinition in social–relational terms. At the same time personal and family problems, often arising through shortcomings in parenting skills, play a decisive role.

So the process of reintegration must balance the personal development of pupil and parents, and changes in their life-style, outlook and skills with the development of an inclusive school culture. Our expectations of pupils are very high, and a small proportion feel themselves falling behind, educationally and socially. These children feel like scapegoats of a system which is insufficiently flexible to cope with them. This is an infrastructural failure, because resources are often tied up in the wrong provision, especially expensive and ineffective special education.

A broad consensus is developing that exclusion, particularly permanent exclusion, is at best a highly unsatisfactory way of dealing with children. The intention to change the situation is there, but 'between the idea and the reality ... falls the shadow' (T.S. Eliot, *The Hollow Men*, 1925). The underlying message in this book is that changes in attitudes, approach, style and awareness are needed, and infrastructural changes should be seen as the mechanism for achieving this, rather than the other way around.

The culture of education is in crisis. Consider the changes over the last 25 years. In the mid-1970s schools were highly individualised places, which taught to an end (the exam syllabus) rather than a means (the curriculum). Parents knew little about the inner workings of the school, or how it compared with others. Teachers managed their own classes in whatever way they saw fit. Many of them were highly committed and worked hard; others did not. They were generally respected by the community, supported by the educational establishment (including teams of inspectors/advisors who also saw themselves in a training and mentoring role), and they managed to hold on to their pupils somehow. We now have a highly prescriptive and barely workable National Curriculum, which undergoes constant structural alterations. OfSTED inspectors require teachers and senior managers to produce extensive planning documents, and tables of exam results which parents and others use to 'compare' schools. Teachers complain of stress and overwork, and are resistant to further demands for more effort. In common with other sections of society, the education culture has become over-scrutinised, over-audited and over-prescribed.

Of course, there were glaring faults with the old system, and many changes over recent years have been for the better. The paragraph above is the briefest possible assessment of a complex area. The fact remains that the strains are now showing and educationalists are wondering: Whither now? What is the role of 'the school in the community'? Who are we and what are we doing, in the wider sense? The technicalities and technology of teaching do not challenge our sense of identity nearly so much as our failures on the pastoral, cultural, and ethological fronts.

Schools need to redefine themselves as multifunctional and multicultural organisations rather than as 'monocultures'. The monocultural approach requires that schools adopt a prescriptive and selective attitude to curriculum and techniques, and especially to the objectives of the school culture – to achieve good GCSE pass-rates. A multifunctional multicultural school will see itself as a 'city', growing organically to meet the needs of its inhabitants, absorbing and accommodating skills and resources (including 'professional skills centres'), and able to include everyone somewhere within its environs. Its objectives are the development of young people into adults. This 'school-city' can operate only within a community which will accommodate it, supported by an establishment which recognises the values of individuality, self-determination and rapid change. Where will the self-confidence to allow such flexibility be found?

There are some useful and comforting parallels to be made here with other professions. Social workers now acknowledge that being in social services' care also carries a high risk. A child may be at risk of harm in the family home, but this has to be compared with the risks associated with being in care, not to a notional 'no-risk' situation. A parallel can be drawn with the response of educationalists to problems in school, where the school is *in loco parentis*. We can afford to acknowledge that whilst increased levels of planning, supervision and statistical accountability may improve practice in one area, practice in another area may be harmed or undervalued. Planning and management become outcomes rather than the agents. Statistical measures become agents rather than indicators. Something may be lost in the process – the intended outcomes.

In essence, control from the centre requires a narrow definition of success and fewer opportunities for self-determination. Increased concern for a narrow measure such as GCSE results means less concern for an alternative measure like exclusion rates. If the DfEE asked pupils directly for their views on the schools they were attending and published these data, what effect would this have on the way the schools functioned? Supervision, auditing and inspection have a place, but they are not the panacea which senior administrators may have thought they would be. So to answer an earlier question, the self-confidence to allow such flexibility can be found in a new realism about the degree to which top-down management can turn schools into the locally responsive centres for child learning and development, within the community, which are the ideal.

Inclusion will increase, as we recognise that we all need to work through fundamental interpersonal issues, especially the primitive impetus to find scapegoats and purify our culture from which exclusion springs. Society and the culture of education will be healthier for it, and our communities more supportive. The power imbalance between schools and pupils should be based on mutual respect and honesty. Schools should be no-blame no-punishment institutions. Discipline and sanctions should be delivered by an accountable and fair system which applies equally to teachers and pupils (just as the law applies to judges and police as well as to the general public). Children who are frequently in trouble should be seen as having special needs, and someone should intervene proactively and find out what the real problems are, and offer real solutions. During days of high stress schoolchildren who are unable to cope should be able to find outlets for their anxiety, and schools should provide and manage a context for this.

In the long term, more efforts and resources to help children at risk of school failure should reduce the cost for the next generation. An inclusive school is providing all of its pupils with a more humane ethos, greater corporate self-esteem and more support. If professionals are given the opportunity to work creatively, flexibly and expansively, it is surprising how quickly the skills base will develop. The challenge is to find affordable ways of delivering effective services. If this did not present difficulties, then services would already be providing it.

Appendix 1: Case studies

The following are all real-life case studies, with the names changed. They illustrate the variety and complexity of the home–school relationship. Readers should use them to facilitate the development of imaginative solutions to current problem pupils, rather than as 'prescriptions for success'.

Lisa – the plump one

Only one visit was made to see Lisa (aged 13) and her mum. She was a sweet and chubby blond girl, the apple of her mother's eye. Problems had arisen for Lisa over one particular subject – Geography, which she was refusing to attend – and because this was not permissible she had been excluded.

Lisa had been insulted by the Geography teacher. As a result she wanted to go into a different Geography group, but this was possible only if she changed tutor groups as well (which the head agreed to). Neither she nor her mother could see why she should have to go through this major change when 'the teacher was at fault'.

I stayed for two hours in the family home, most of which was spent sympathising with Lisa in her troubles. The truth was, the teacher had insulted her figure, and Lisa was very sensitive about this. The mother eventually confided in me that she too had been taunted about her size in school. The teacher had found a weak spot and had jabbed at it, by making egotistical comments in front of the whole class. Mum wanted something done. After 90 minutes of listening, empathising and commiserating, mother and daughter were mollified.

Both now accepted the following logic. Lisa would not want to go back into the class with the teacher under any circumstances. The only way to change the geography teacher was to change tutor groups. A formal complaint about the teacher could still be pursued after Lisa had agreed to change tutor groups. Lisa duly started back at school on the following Monday.

■ Erita – repressed but defiant

Erita was another young lady who was self-conscious about her figure, but she was altogether a more mature and outward-going person than Lisa. Her problem was her father. But for father read 'father and culture'.

Mr Yaissa was an impeccable and well-mannered Muslim businessman, who knew he would be returning to his home country in due course. His children, however, had grown up in the UK and had British attitudes. Erita's sister accepted her father and his demanding attitude. But the more emotional Erita fought him every inch of the way. She claimed to hate him, and his unreasonableness.

The school reported that Erita was truanting, and coming into conflict with one of the more rigid and autocratic male teachers. The danger signs were obvious. The tasks were to help Erita to find out why she went out of class, why she felt the need to have conflict with the teacher, to find strategies to help her cope with her father, and to persuade the father to adopt a more realistic approach to his responsibilities, before Erita took the law into her own hands and ran away, or was excluded.

Erita was happy to talk to me, and we met for five or six sessions over two months. I also saw her father on two occasions and talked to him on the telephone. I was an outlet for her feelings of anger, and a source of encouragement and advice. Her conflict with the male teacher was soon resolved – she simply had to picture him as a small boy having a tantrum, and smile when he was being stroppy. We discussed separating his behaviour from hers. She didn't have to respond to him when he is like that. She understood, on reflection, that for all his faults he was an honourable and well-meaning person. She did not realize how quickly he felt undermined by cheeky pupils, until I explained it to her.

By listening, empathising and accepting what Erita said, I was able to build up her trust and confidence in me. It was clear that she felt she could not achieve as highly as her older sister, and it was her anxiety about failure which made her want to escape school. Whenever she said something about her father's attitude, I asked her whether he had actually said these things, or she had simply imagined he would. Once challenged by her, he turned out to be much more reasonable about her efforts than she had anticipated. However, on one thing he was intransigent – she was going to be an engineer, whether she liked it or not. As a matter of fact, she did not like it, preferring to be a musician.

At the meetings we had together I listened carefully to what Mr Yaissa had to say. I sympathised with him too. He was a man of integrity and intelligence. He would have enjoyed a dutiful and obedient daughter, but he did not have one. I reminded him that the first words of the Koran were: 'In the name of Allah, the *compassionate*, the *merciful*'. I asked him to think compassionately about his daughter, and I also reassured him. Erita had more of her father in her than she realised, and her views and aspirations would change. Meanwhile, it did no harm for her to dream of being a musician.

Mr Yaissa took a great cultural leap into the dark for the sake of his daughter. It must have been tough for him to relax his vigilant resistance to the materialism of western society, and the relative freedom of women. He was hard on her, but she was hard on him, too. But he was first to begin to think in terms of compromise, and to Erita's surprise told her that she could be a musician if she wanted. He also agreed to her going out in the evenings (with some less restrictive conditions). Erita was slower to reciprocate, but at this point I was able to cash in my credit with her.

'Erita, you know I have listened to what you have said, and you know I have supported your point of view, and spoken to the teachers and your father on your behalf. I have always believed you, and stuck up for you. Now I am saying – this time it's you. You have to make a move now. You know your father is trying and so is the school. Now you have to meet everybody half way.'

Bunking lessons seems to have stopped and there have been no in-school negative referrals since the programme started.

▨ The story of Hassan – and an unexpected ally

Hassan's reintegration into secondary school, following his exclusion from Year 6, is a testimony to the power of the family group conference process to change family dynamics and school behaviour.

Hassan was excluded in the last year of his primary school for defiant and disruptive behaviour, very unpleasant verbal abuse, and fighting. He was apparently overheard saying he was going to rape Mandy, the teacher. Faced with an instruction he did not like, he used to say 'I don't have to do that, if I don't want.'

He had an older brother, three older sisters, and a younger brother and sister. The eldest girl (Soraya, 21 years) had been taken into care following claims of physical abuse, and the brother was in prison at the time of referral. I went to the house on two occasions (sampling his mother's superb Arab baking) before forming an impression of the way forward. However, I quickly discovered that there was no common language in the family!! One exclamation mark is insufficient to convey the sense of shock and disbelief this aroused. Surely, this must have been a critical factor in the equation. And yet, despite a substantial file which included at least one KS3 (SENCoP) educational psychologist's assessment, this fact was unrecorded! Both parents spoke and understood a little basic English, but the father, especially when upset, could hardly articulate at all. The children did not know enough Tunisian Arabic to talk in depth to their parents. Clearly, while small talk was just possible, nothing of the least importance could ever be said by parents to children, or vice versa. There were also a number of other cultural barriers between the two generations (especially over pop culture, and teenage socialising). Father had a heart problem.

It was Soraya who brought Hassan for the office meeting, and filled in the assessment inventories. It was she who spoke maturely and at length about his difficulties, and stressed that he needed extra help with explanations. Hassan looked up to her, and turned to her for guidance on even the simplest of my questions. This was the person who had most influence on Hassan's behaviour. Over the next few weeks Soraya filled in many of the gaps in his story with the help of her mother. Soraya had been taken into care, to protect her from the violence of her father. After Soraya had achieved a degree of independence, she returned on condition that he left her to do as she wished, and her father appeared to accept this. She saw herself as protector and guide to her siblings, and frequently came between them and their father's anger.

Social services and the psychotherapy service were involved, but disagreed about the best course of action. Social services were clear that they could do little to prevent the adolescent girls, Walida and Aisha, from staying out late and apparently getting into dubious involvements with men. They wanted the psychotherapists to work with the family. The social worker wanted Soraya to learn to accept her parent's authority, but did not know how to bring this about. The psychotherapists wanted social services to get a court order to prevent Walida and Aisha (who ironically were also close to permanent exclusion because of their non-attendance) from visiting certain houses in the neighbourhood which had ill-repute. Their big idea was that the family should change so that the younger children did not feel they had to go through the process of rebellion, care and return which Soraya had.

The problem for the psychotherapists was that only the mother was turning up for their sessions. The social services did not think that the court order would be enforceable, and would not apply for it. The perceptions of both agencies were sound so far as they went. The problem was that nothing was changing.

The family dynamics were sketched out on a single sheet of paper, as an aid to thinking. The family was badly split on cultural language lines. On the one side were parents and younger children, who would eventually drift over to the other side if history were allowed to repeat

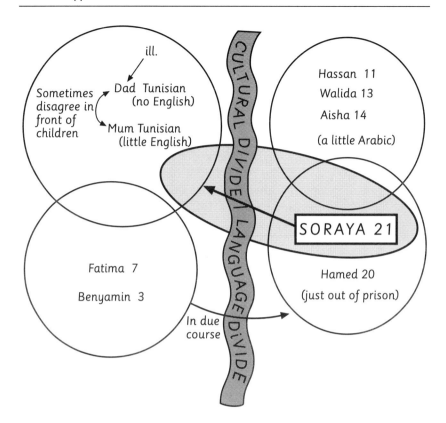

itself. On the other side were five older children: Hamed, rather sad, dope-smoker, ex-con at twenty, and looking for a job; the three adolescent children, close to social failure and delinquency; and Soraya. She was the most powerful figure in the family. The big black arrow in the middle of the sketch is the movement that Soraya needed to make, crossing the divide and reuniting the family. She needed to work with her parents, not as a subject but as an equal.

The current level of conflict in the family was deeply disturbing to Hassan, and he took this upset into school with him, where it would spill into many situations. He was frequently tired, preoccupied with family problems, and perhaps felt alienated by his ambiguous cultural background. He may also have had some cognitive limitations in understanding instructions. He doted on Soraya, who rather naively thought that what worked in life for her should work for everyone, and told him that 'You don't have to do things, if you don't want to.'

The first objective was a family group conference to reduce the level of family discord. Secondly, if Soraya could understand her role in Hassan's success and learn to support him in the right way, a key element in

Hassan's world would have been changed for the better. Her parents seemed happy to relinquish responsibility in her favour. Over a period of time an important relationship was developed with Soraya, through which this understanding could be shared. We used to meet in the pub near the newsagent where she worked, and at first she would only say: *'Nothing can change, no-one can do anything.'* Eventually she came to understand that she could 'change the message'.

Seventeen people attended the family group conference (FGC). The psychotherapist admitted afterwards that it was the first time she had seen all the family together. Professionals are excluded from the planning part of a family group conference. We waited outside and, after about 45 minutes, Soraya stormed out, with all the children in tow. Tears flowed. Children were up and down stairs, shouting excitedly. The crisis had been reached, and here on neutral territory the choice before her was starkly outlined: to take the children back in, or to take them away ... where? She looked at me and said: *'I can't be responsible for all these children. I love them, but I just can't cope with them all.'* She returned to the room, and she and her parents began to explore this new beginning.

Hassan returned to a new primary school for the last half-term of Year 6, and then transferred to a local secondary school. At the first half-term review the school's assessment was that no support was needed, and that although they had some concerns over his learning weaknesses, they saw no need to apply for the Statement which the local authority had suggested to them.

The story of Imran – family disaster, followed by services catastrophe!

Imran had to understand, assimilate and reconcile himself to a catalogue of disasters, and then to manage the relationships and life-style which went with them. These disasters included the disintegration of his family, separation from his older sisters, the chronic alcoholism of his mother, the lack of fathering provided by his father, repeated breakdowns in fostering arrangements, the disruptive effect of transfer by the social services department from his own locality to another London borough and then back again, the consequent lack of a school, and a long period in a short-stay council-run children's home set up as an assessment centre mainly for immigrants and refugees.

Imran often managed to smile and was generally well-mannered and sociable. It was as if he devoted most of his energy to the task of maintaining his self-respect and identity in the face of multiple circumstantial onslaughts. His mother lived in a squalid doss-house, and his father had a well-paid job as a broadcaster. Neither they nor his older siblings were willing or able to form the nucleus for even a partial reunion of the family. Social services were unable to formulate an effective plan, partly because the managers of the case were 'old-style' social workers with 'engineering mentalities'. Instead of working with Imran's obvious and clearly expressed need to be close to his mother and to visit her at regular intervals, they decided the relationship was 'unhealthy' and did everything they could to break it, including fostering Imran in a distant borough, miles from all that was familiar to him – including his home, locality and his friends.

Blood ties proved stronger than professional will. His mother's alcoholism had destroyed the family, and his father's inadequacies prevented him from filling the gap. His social worker's folly ensured that Imran was condemned to a nomadic and evasive existence. His schooling was simply a casualty in the crossfire, and throughout the five months during which Imran was waiting to hear where he would be moved he would not attend the school found for him. He did not want to form a link with a school until he knew where he would live, a reasonable position to adopt. In the end he did move some distance away, which would have necessitated a long journey had he taken up the place. As a 14-year-old, he clearly had a right to have his wishes considered. His social worker kept looking for a place further away from mother, and he kept rejecting these options. In the end social services gave in, and found him a foster family within travelling distance of his old home.

Imran used all his emotional energy to preserve his identity, and maintain for most of the time an extraordinary balance of mind, good manners and general civility. Over time he did become more delinquent, buying 'weed' to smoke, stealing petty cash when he was broke, and breaking house rules when it suited him. He often had to lie about his movements, and the stress took its toll. These things were completely normal under the circumstances.

Imran's emotional state made it nearly impossible for him to hold down a school place. The anxiety, uncertainty and insecurity he was experiencing placed a considerable strain on him; he slept badly and was tired, he was frustrated by the disparity between his own agenda and the 'hidden' agenda of the social workers. His life was interrupted by unnatural events such as visits to potential foster-carers in far corners of the city, and attendance at planning meetings and reviews. He frequently missed tuition sessions provided whilst he was out of school, because he wanted to visit his mother. In addition, his identity was consequently under threat, necessitating a state of vigilance; after all, he was not living in circumstances which might ordinarily be considered as 'home'. Under these circumstances which of us would be able to go to work on a daily basis and concentrate, especially without the availability of the escape mechanisms to which adult workers typically resort?

▧ Nathan and Simon – two boys, one story

These two pupils shared similar backgrounds, the same glaringly obvious problem, and mothers who refused at first to accept the simple solution. As such, they were exceptions to the rule that no two cases are the same.

Each lived in a family of three people with a single-parent working mother and an older sibling. Both were excluded from co-educational schools for disruptive behaviour, especially out of class, and for inappropriate behaviour with girls. As one governor put it, at Nathan's exclusion appeal, 'They lead you on, and wind you up, and you can't help yourself.' A single-sex school would remedy the problem, but neither mother would accept this at first.

Nathan's problem was that he was good-looking, and easily aroused and frustrated. The girls flirted with him but he did not know when to stop. On occasion he had even followed them into the toilets. He took the flirting too seriously and wanted to make something of it, which created anxiety and then a counter-reaction from the girls. He also verbally abused girls who had seemed to offend him in some way. His attitude to younger female teachers was unsatisfactory. There were a number of out-of-class conflicts which reflected badly on him, although the records seldom showed how the incidents arose. Simon was slower and lazier, but although the scenarios were different the root cause was similar. His record describes how girls complained of not liking his staring, or his veiled invitations to get physically involved. One report talked of him breathing on a girl's neck.

The reports suggested that these boys were oversexed and lacked self-control. Their stories raise numerous issues – for instance, the sexuality of young black men, role models and chauvinism, Oedipal relationships in single-parent families, and possible dysfunctional relationships in three-person family groups with dominant mothers. In an ideal world of limitless resources, and if either mother had been amenable to involvement in family counselling or therapy, these issues might have been addressed. In practice, the simple expedient of finding an all-boys school was sufficient. Both pupils ended up in the same school and both made a success of it.

The other story about Nathan

Nathan's mother, Teresa, flatly refused to allow her son to go to an all-boys school, and I therefore found him a local church school from which he was permanently excluded for a second time. Under the new regulations (1998) this would effectively have barred him from any mainstream school, although in his third secondary school he was very successful.

The church school could have made a better job of managing him, in that they did not provide clear boundaries and a firm disciplinary structure. The only sanction levied on Nathan during his three months at the school was his permanent exclusion. Without clearly imposed boundaries he was at a loss to understand his limitations. Nathan and his parents went to the exclusion meeting under the impression that a 'contract' was to be suggested. However, the head teacher responded to Teresa's untimely demand to know whether he was going to permanently exclude Nathan with a peremptory 'Yes!' This triggered an explosive verbal attack, in which she accused him of racism. Her subsequent rampage through the school looking for the teacher who had triggered the situation did not improve the chances of a successful appeal.

The pupil was punished for the behaviour of the mother! However, she was quite right to reject the request by the local authority to have a formal psychological assessment. This knee-jerk reaction demonstrates how institutions can reach for procedural life-rafts in the absence of any real initiatives. Within two weeks he had been found a place in a school which provided the firm behavioural structure he needed, and no girls! He stayed there until the age of 16 (for three more years).

The other story about Simon

Simon's mother, Sarah, was very upset by the rejection of her child. She had been excluded from secondary school herself, and when Simon had started at this self-same school she was shocked one day to meet one of her old teachers who remembered her and the exclusion.

What mixed feelings such a meeting must have engendered became apparent when she took Simon away from the school because she was frightened that he would get 'tarred with the same brush'. She found him a new school and told them that she had removed Simon because she was worried that history might repeat itself. She asked them to keep this information confidential. Imagine her *chagrin* when Simon told her that his teacher had said in front of the class: 'You left your previous school because you were going to get excluded like your mum, didn't you!'

History did repeat itself, and Simon came to the reintegration programme. He should probably never have left his first school. He wasn't much interested in an out-of-school programme. He wanted to go back to school, and he clearly felt there was not much he had done wrong except to be big and black, with a reputation, and to have been interested in the wrong girls, in the wrong way.

Like Teresa, Sarah wanted her son to have the benefit of mixing with girls. The problem was that their sons weren't just mixing, they were mixing it! How many boys are there in the UK who have been excluded from co-educational schools, and who would have behaved perfectly well in an all-boys school, given the chance?

▨ The story of Aleem – the boy who turned himself (with a little help)

Aleem was permanently excluded on the last day of the summer term for 'taking a bunch of keys and refusing to hand them back'. He lived near his school, with his chronically arthritic mother (and younger brother). There was a very close and caring relationship between the two. His stepfather lived-in on a part-time basis. His mother revealed to me at our third meeting that she had attended a special school, and then a secure unit. Aleem frequently asked to go home because of mysterious stomach pains or headaches. His misdemeanours consisted mainly of naughtiness (e.g. setting off the fire alarm), arguing, and refusing to carry out some tasks in class.

Aleem was very concerned about his mother's health (she sometimes passed out unexpectedly, or was bed-bound). He said he thought she would get better – but she said 'that's not what the doctor says'). He was preoccupied by thoughts of death, and mentioned seeing the body of a suicide. He was very preoccupied at times with the possibility of a fire. He admitted that his vague illnesses were a ploy to allow him to go home and check his mother's well-being. Eventually he simply acknowledged that he had wanted to be excluded.

Two social deficits were apparent in a class situation. The first was a 'scrutiny phobia' which manifested itself as an aversion to activities in which Aleem was the centre of attention (reading aloud, at the front of the class, answering questions, drama, and so on). A slight speech impediment would have exacerbated this. (As a result he had a strong aversion to French lessons, especially where they involved oral tasks.) The second was his truculent obstinacy when required to do this sort of activity, or indeed anything which he thought was 'too difficult'. Teachers with an insensitive or confrontational style would have had problems coping with this.

Aleem needed speech therapy, a strategy for reducing his anxiety over mother, a moderation of his aversion to French. He also needed to learn how to manage difficult situations in school more appropriately. This plan would also have the effect of building his confidence and self-esteem.

Speech therapy was arranged by GP referral. Bringing his mother-anxiety into open discussion led to his eventual mastery of the problem. We seriously considered providing him with a pager on his return to school, so that his mother could confirm her wellbeing at regular intervals, with a view to phasing this out over time as its reassuring effect became conditioned to events in the school day (a 'high-tech' behavioural programme). However, events conspired to help us. His mother made a new friend in the same block of flats. Aleem believed she would 'keep an eye' on mother. There was probably also a beneficial effect of maturation which was seen, in a number of cases, to mitigate a range of problems. We sometimes forget that to an adolescent a term represents a significant proportion of time in his or her personal history.

At regular meetings role-play and rational–emotive therapy were used to boost his self-confidence by challenging the unhelpful aspects of his approach to schooling. For instance, a teacher play-acted accusing him of talking when he hadn't. Aleem persisted in arguing, and so was 'sent out', and when he refused to go the head was called. Then, the irritable and hard-pressed head gave Aleem the exclusion he had earned himself! This was great fun but Aleem also began to realise how he had provoked problems for himself. On subsequent occasions he learned how to say 'yes sir', 'no sir', and later to complain to his tutor 'in the right way', if he felt mistreated. Aleem was also told that all the staff would be asked to watch him dance on the table and sing a song. Aleem was never quite sure whether this was a serious suggestion, but the image served as a way of safely exposing his worst fears, in order to desensitise them.

French became the substantial feature of his tuition timetable, with the objective of reducing his dislike of it, and his anxieties about it. At first he refused to co-operate but the reintegration team were the gatekeepers to his new school and he had no option but to do so. He proved to have a very good accent and pronunciation, which his slight speech impediment enhanced, and positive feedback was profuse. After a few sessions he appeared to start enjoying it!

Aleem was very keen to get back to school and this acted as a powerful lever in helping him to change. As his outlook changed, so his confidence increased. Aleem needed to separate himself emotionally from his mother, and he was provided with a week-long respite break on a Norfolk farm which reinforced new feelings of independence. This would have been the first time Aleem spent a significant amount of time away from his mother. His carer there reported that he was obsessed with the price of everything, and thought all the furniture was antique (it was just old!). She found him nervous and afraid of the dark, and thought 'he needed toughening up'. She found him a local playmate and, significantly, by the end of the week he had adjusted to playing around the farm after dark without a torch.

Meanwhile, work with his mother to reduce the risk of collusion in school-avoidance strategies was facilitated by her positive attitude. Any delay in returning to school is considered unhelpful in school-phobia programmes. However, in the case of permanent exclusion other issues arise. The long delay must be turned to advantage, acting as a buffer, reducing the impact of traumatic memories and feelings associated with the exclusion, and providing maturation time. Motivation to return to school increases as boredom sets in, and loneliness bringing into focus aspects of school life which are sorely missed, raising the global value of school.

Two weeks after his return to school his mother phoned. Aleem was saying he wouldn't go back to school. He was being 'threatened by a whole group of big boys'. One of them 'had a huge machete hidden in his trousers' which he had threatened Aleem with. The boys were not from the school, and he couldn't say what they looked like because 'they were hooded'. His mother was clearly feeling very protective, and was reminded of all that had gone on before and of Aleem's tendency to become over-anxious about school. Aleem was reassured that his complaint would be investigated. Mother agreed to do everything in her power to persuade him to go to school, and to ask his stepfather to take him in. But something suddenly 'clicked' for Aleem. He took the phone back and said with new confidence: 'I will be going to school on Monday.' On other occasions similar problems arose, but Aleem eventually settled down and made good use of his intelligence.

Ricky and Scott – old before their time?

These two cases have much in common. Both are stories of young men who declined to attend. They both could have made a success of their reintegration. They both rejected school, one because he had a better offer (regular work in the market) and did not expect to succeed at GCSE. The other appeared to have simply outgrown the culture. Ricky expressed something very important about values and the right to choose. Scott's family culture makes his case exemplary – a classic of its kind.

Ricky

Ricky was bullied by his brothers for much of his childhood. It seemed to be the way that problems were managed in the family. On the other hand the family's simple 'code of practice' was supported by a good deal of cohesion and love. As a result Ricky had developed a remarkabe personal psychology.

Ricky had two states of mind (other than 'calm') and two responses to these states. If he was 'quite annoyed' with someone, honour required that he verbally insult them. If he was 'very annoyed' the strategy was to hit them. Ricky seemed to believe he could get by with these clear guidelines, and expressed surprise that a more sophisticated approach to others might be needed. This was his family's way.

Ricky saw fit to knock out a policeman who (no doubt unjustifiably) was harassing him. He claimed that the other policemen involved had said their colleague deserved it. Ricky's parents, while regretting that the incident had occurred, were clearly of the view that if someone gets you 'very annoyed', then the correct thing to do is to hit them, regardless of the consequences. Ricky's father described similar incidents in which he had been involved. He was not a bad character, and did his best to find work as a lorry driver. In every way this immensely likeable family were good-natured and co-operative, respectful and well-mannered. Their greatest fault was not of their making – they were bone-poor. Obviously, I took care never to annoy them!

This approach to life extended to school. Ricky felt he had been picked on, and there may have been over-reaction on the part of some teachers (Ricky was a big lad who would have been quite intimidating, especially to more vulnerable teachers). His behaviour had been inappropriate. We discussed the question of natural justice and social norms: whose agenda had been better served by his behaviour? When Ricky had felt unfairly told off, he had stood up and roundly abused the teacher.

> *'But Ricky, you got excluded and missed your lessons ... and the teacher still got paid – who lost out?'*
> *'Yes, but I made him feel a fool in front of class.'*
> *'And now you're out of school. But you've said the one school you would like to go to is the one from which your actions caused you to be excluded.'*
> *'Yes, but I made him feel a fool in front of the class!'*

Ricky really was saying, in his own way, that the consequences of an action are not the only valid criteria for deciding what is right. In one way, this was a highly principled and heroic outlook on life, and it was logically very difficult to shift. Ricky felt good because he had shown up the fool of a teacher, and he had done the right thing. When challenged to say whether he thought there was a problem with his anger, he was saying there wasn't. No problem – no change.

Ricky was a likeable young man with a likeable family, and he was often misguided and ended up in court on several occasions. But it is difficult to describe him as bad, and impossible to describe him as a schoolboy. He just matured too early.

Scott

Scott (15 years old) was a large and not unprepossessing young man with a listless and reluctant manner. He had been excluded for a series of disruptive and defiant incidents and abusive language. His father had tried hard to overturn the school's decision, to no avail.

Scott didn't like school at all and said so. He lacked motivation and had few interests, with the exception of a casual job in the market (for which he was well paid). He kept out of trouble outside school. His father, Geoff, was rather domineering, especially in meetings. Scott had many anxieties and fears (for instance about being bullied) although he was strongly built. He disliked violent images. In tuition sessions the teachers reported a reluctance or refusal to work.

Scott's mother was a very poor carer and nurturer both emotionally and physically, who failed to provide for the infant Scott adequately, leaving when Scott was six. His aunt described how she had found him standing crying in the garden in winter, nearly naked, whilst his mother lay in bed watching television. Scott had a very negative reaction to young female teachers, which might have related to feelings about his mother. It disrupted one-to-one sessions and in-class support after reintegration. After Scott's mother left, his father tried to make up for his lack of parenting skills by lavish treats.

The family dynamics were complicated by the arrival of Iris (his second wife), who had a much clearer idea of domestic propriety and cleanliness, but her involvement was a secondary loss for Scott because he was displaced from the superior place in his father's affections. His younger brother Terry, on the other hand, who had been marginalised by the older and more demanding Scott, now enjoyed a greater degree of affection from both father and stepmother. It was no surprise to find out that Terry was doing well at home and school. Whilst Scott was a very neglected only-child for several years, Terry had always had an older brother, if only to show him how to open the fridge.

Geoff's sympathies were split between his wife who frequently became unreasonable and hysterical, and his son who frequently undermined family life (by creating problems in school, or at home, for instance by stealing). Geoff's parenting strategies were limited, and extreme sanctions (such as confining Scott to his bedroom *'indefinitely'*) soon broke down as the onerous task of maintaining them took its toll. Geoff's approach was over-assertive and bombastic. His dogmatic statements were not designed for negotiation. The scripts which Scott heard repeatedly were like this:

- ▪ *'I am blameless and powerless'*
- communicated by periods of resigned apathy during which Scott would be told

'I couldn't care less what you do'
'I just can't take any more'
'I've done everything I can and things are still no good';

- ▪ *'You are also blameless and powerless'*
- communicated by periods of righteous anger during which Scott would be told

'The school is negligent'
'The teachers are incompetent'
'You need help that you are not getting';

- ▪ *'You are a disgusting and revolting waste of space'*
- communicated in a wide variety of phrases, in words very similar to those;

- ▪ *'You are so bad that I am going to punish you severely'*
- communicated by threats of expulsion from the family home, draconian sentences such as 'grounded for six months', and other horrible fulminating regimes;

- ▪ *'Only joking!'*
- communicated by the inevitable collapse of stout party.

Iris meanwhile communicated a different set of ambivalent and mixed messages, and the emotional charge arising from Scott's many misdemeanours was amplified by Geoff who often tried to conceal things from her, in case it plunged her into despair again.

In such a complex situation the clients' needs were well beyond the remit of a single worker. To refer to an outside agency is an easy, but not necessarily a sufficient, action – especially if the family concerned will not respond. Since Iris had relapsed again and was taking medication for most of the time, Geoff was more amenable to outside influence. The opportunity arose to refer to an Art therapist. Geoff and Scott were persuaded to agree to this. Surprisingly, Geoff was also prepared to reconsider family therapy. The family were referred as quickly as possible.

Family therapy could have enabled Scott to assert his own view of the situation, and redress the imbalance between Iris' view and his. A third party could have enabled Geoff to move away from the split roles of alliances with opposing camps. Terry's needs and feelings could modify the dynamics positively if they were be expressed safely. Access to improved strategies and support would help Geoff to manage two adolescent boys and an unwell wife more effectively. But Iris had by now recovered and was too resourceful in finding Scott a place in a school, which not surprisingly broke down. Scott needed some months during which the Art therapy could start to bring about changes in his outlook. Regrettably, Iris could not accept the need for family therapy.

Geoff fell back on the classic rejoinder: *'Why should we all go to therapy when Scott is the one causing all the problem!'* As usual Iris' influence was paramount. Likewise, over the summer holiday, Scott's art therapy folded. Iris said: *'We think it is upsetting him, by bringing it all to the surface.'* This was a sign that the Art therapy was working, but the need to find a scapegoat was overwhelming. In the autumn term Scott, under threat of re-exclusion, was transferred to the college-based course. The situation had returned almost to its starting point, but hopefully along the way some insights had been shared and absorbed.

Scott's reintegration was not a success. However, had he come earlier to the programme the outcome might have been different. Geoff was an inadvertent saboteur, and we did not know how to stop him. He decided that the Art therapy was 'a waste of time' and told Scott as much, and after the failure of the second school place he seemed strangely comforted when he said: *'I told Scott that I would give it until Christmas, if that, before he's out again.'* Surely this was a self-fulfilling prophecy. Scott wanted to go back to work in the market as he had done during the long summer holiday, and he viewed exclusion as an opportunity to do so. True to form, Geoff was determined to prevent this happening.

There is something neurotic about labelling a pupil as 'in need of treatment' when all he really wanted to do was leave school and go to work. In some parts of Europe pupils of his age are at liberty to do just that. In some ways Scott showed a kind of courage in trying to do what he wanted in spite of the pressures arising from two separate and different examples of flawed parenthood, and the demands of an uncomprehending society. His methods were, however, devious and his inability to trust others was unhelpful.

▓▓▓ The story of Raymond – a textbook assessment

Raymond's exclusion at the beginning of Year 8 (aged 12) resulted from his use of abusive language, disruptive behaviour, failure to keep within accepted boundaries, and aggression. Raymond was the son of an overburdened young single mother, abandoned by her children's father, struggling to hold down a job and hold up her head. The underlying problem was the high level of criticism and low level of warmth in her parenting style. Raymond was correspondingly stressed and oversensitive to criticism.

Martha claimed never to have given Raymond a hug, and never to have been hugged by her own mother. She had never told her son she loved him (although she could tell me). She had never read to him or heard him read, but seemed genuinely keen to do what she could to help.

The following depressing sequence of events was also important:

- Four years previously his primary school had referred him to the educational psychology department because of concerns at his poor social skills, inability to take responsibility for his actions, and excessive emotional reactions. A possible specific language difficulty was suggested. Nothing else was done.

- Later, a speech therapist, finding no organic cause but noting the disparity between his oral and written skills, recommended a remedial programme. However nothing effective was done.

- By the time of his exclusion he had a serious literacy deficit, although his level of achievement in maths was well above average.

A reading test showed that Raymond was using his high level of intelligence to read by guessing from semantic and other cues. This method becomes less effective as texts become more complex, and is more stressful. When tested it was clear that he had important basic gaps in his phonetic understanding. He began the SRA literacy programme for decoding skills and his grandmother was asked to help with his reading. She also helped him with the SRA programme, along with the teachers. This literacy work formed the core of his education programme throughout his time on the project.

The Child Behaviour Checklist (Achenbach, 1974) proved exceptionally powerful in Raymond's case, because of the similarities and contrasts between the responses of Raymond and his mother. When asked to 'describe the best things about your son (/myself)', neither could think of anything to write, even after several minutes.

On the anxiety scale, their scores were almost identical. But Raymond said he felt lonely and guilty, and his mother had no idea about this. Raymond also feared he would do bad things but didn't believe people were out to get him; but his mother held the opposite view. Finally, his mother said he worried a lot, but Raymond said he did not.

- Martha knew that someone was 'out to get Raymond' – *she felt it was herself*. Raymond didn't see this and felt guilty instead.

- Of course, the mother assumed Raymond didn't feel guilty because she knew he wasn't – *she felt guilty instead!*

- Raymond was highly criticised ('I have to be perfect at home because I am in trouble because of my little sister, and my mum gives me a hard time') and *thought worrying was a normal state.*

- He didn't even realize that what he did all the time was worrying – his mother's insight here was better.

Socially, Raymond was struggling emotionally, but because his mother and he couldn't talk she never knew this. She had stopped his one after-school social activity, which he loved, as a punishment for getting excluded. He thought he was too dependent on adults – probably because his mother always pushed him away. She never knew how teased he felt, because he couldn't share it with her. His father, who lived away from the family, had also rejected him, by way of punishment.

Raymond was brought up in a highly critical environment with little affection, making him oversensitive. His anxieties stemmed from the lack of warmth and security he experienced particularly as a young child. He had always had to fight to get any attention from his busy mother. He became aggressive, and feelings of guilt made him excessively defensive. Educationally his poor literacy skills reduced self-esteem still further. An intelligent boy, he sought to cover up his perceived inadequacies.

It is always a delicate matter to share critical insights with a family member. Meetings with Martha took place at home, at the project base, and at her place of work. Martha began to feel someone was on her side. She told her life story – of how she had become pregnant as a teenager (the father abandoning her) and how her mother had thrown her out; of her life in bed and breakfast accommodation with a baby; and of how she had struggled to get a flat and a job (she was now a medical receptionist). History had repeated itself a decade later as her partner left her before the birth of her daughter. There was something almost heroic about her achievements against these odds. But her style of parenting was as cold as that of her mother. She knew what was wrong but didn't know how to change. The level of domestic conflict, the way the children fought, and her despair were key issues. Finding solutions is generally easier than acknowledging problems and the difficult part was over. A plan was made for Martha, and reviewed after a few weeks:

- Give Raymond a chance to talk, away from Sasha (his sister).

- Learn just to listen.

- Don't try to justify yourself if he needs to be critical of you.

- Give him cues that it is safe to talk about his feelings.

- Start with neutral topics.

- Let the bad things come out first and then you will hear the good things.

- Do it again, do it regularly!

On coping with two children at once:

- Give both children hugs and kisses.

- Separate them by being with them.

- Sit down between them and get Raymond to read to Sasha while you cuddle both.

- Remember that if children get your attention only when they are bad, then they will go on being bad!

On rewards:

- Give small immediate rewards for being good.

- Think of things for one to do while the other helps you in the kitchen.

- Give them masses of praise.

- Show them that what they do is good enough and that they are good enough.

- *Tell* them you love them.

The last item was something we laughed over many times; the joke being that she couldn't tell her own children she loved them. I explained how to say the words without making it a big deal. Every time we spoke I asked her if she had done this yet – she always said no, but she said one day soon she would – she could feel it coming! At the same time youth support workers were helping Raymond find things he could excel at, and something he could say he did well: his Maths work, his basketball, his drawing.

He was given a ten-day break in Scotland staying with a family in the Western Isles, and then went into school. He started off too confidently for his own good. He still had a tendency to argue, and one teacher very unfairly refused to teach him at all, because he had been rude to her. She kept this up, quite unjustifiably, for half a term. However, on balance the school got it right, picking up on everything he did wrong and making him review it for himself. A supportive form teacher and a skilled head-of-year ensured that Raymond was drawn into a commitment to the school.

A key issue was whether Martha was sending him to school in a positive frame of mind. On one day which was a particular problem (as the school reported) she acknowledged that she had been horrible to him that morning. But she had had to get up early and have the 8-year-old dressed and fed, ready to go to her grandmother's by seven-thirty so that she could leave for work. Raymond had to leave the house a few minutes later; and the strain on all of them was immense. She needed to make Raymond responsible for himself, and not get on his back from the moment they woke up. He was old enough to do this, and she needed to learn to relax, and just let him do it for himself. One result of this was that she did not feel obliged to harass him in the mornings.

▨ The story of John the poet, damaged but not beyond repair

John was quite disturbed, and intervention late in the day had only a limited effect on him. He would probably have benefited from a period in a therapeutic community. He did manage to hold down a school place for nine months, but started to non-attend before his mock GCSEs and never returned to sit his final GCSE examinations.

John's mother also had some mental health difficulties. She was pleasant and well-mannered, but the flatness in her voice and lack of facial expression were signs of the depressive illness she struggled against. She was also an intensely private person, and it was all too easy to overstep her personal boundaries, which made us both rather tense, at first.

Welfare social services were already involved and providing support. There had also been a good deal of input from a Family Therapy Centre and counselling from an Educational Welfare Officer.

As often happens, one twin seemed younger than the other; in this case it was James, who was doing well at school. John was probably carrying most of the emotional load for the family. His permanent exclusion followed a string of incidents involving bad temper, emotional outbursts and aggressive conflict with teachers. He was a very bright boy who could achieve really well at school but he struggled emotionally, being oversensitive and lacking self-awareness. His key problem was anger.

It was a struggle at first to persuade him to accept that he did have problems and needed to deal with them. He had great difficulty expressing his feelings verbally, but was able to write poems as a vehicle to explore the links between feelings and actions:

The fizzy drink.
There he is,
Make sure you don't
Shake him up and open his
Lid, then you will be sorry.

This powerful image is not hard to understand, and we returned to it again and again. John had also created his own concept of 'the provoker'. Petrol was leaking (we were not sure where from), and for obvious reasons it was important not to disturb it. The provoker was 'matchstick'. The inevitable result was 'a raging fire' which 'makes people sorry', although because they had ignored the sign on the door saying 'do not enter' they really only had themselves to blame. We discussed how to manage the petrol more safely – for instance by safely burning off small amounts of petrol.

Another poem he wrote is more enigmatic:

Why, why, why, why, me, me, me,
What makes people see such cruelty,
I'm a boy and you are a provoker ...
How dare you, How dare he,
Keep trying to provoke me.
Oh, I ought to get a great sharp thing,
And strike you down until you're as thin
As paper.
But I say no! Can you guess why?
Because I don't want to see you cry ...

Imagery must be translated back into a real-world context if it is to inform action. John gradually learned how to assess his state of mind before deciding how to act, though a great deal remained unexpressed. John had disclosed his fear of insanity and described some odd perceptions of colour and light which troubled him.

▓▓ Shane's story – well, his mother's really

Shane was excluded from an independent boarding school, to which the authority had sent him because he had been chronically bullied at his primary school. This very unusual step was taken, to persuade his very determined mother not to sue for damages.

Shane was an easy-going boy who felt socially way out of his depth amongst pupils, saying 'their parents arrive in Jaguars'. His mother lived alone, and Shane was concerned about her wellbeing particularly, in view of the emotionally abusive relationship she had with her egotistical boyfriend. Shane wanted to get back home, and frankly, that suited the school too. In particular, one teacher had a clearly racist motivation in blatantly telling Shane he was not wanted at the school (sadly, such statements are not a unique occurrence).

Shane's mother, Kirsty, had had a uniquely difficult childhood. She and her sister had been brought up by their alcoholic father when the mother deserted them. Her sister blamed her for her father's eventual suicide. Her mother's subsequent nurturing of the children was barely adequate, and Kirsty grew up guilty and emotionally neglected, with unresolved grief for her father and little encouragement to succeed. But after a manner she did succeed, and lived in reasonable comfort with Shane.

Shane needed less help than the mother, and was well above average in both ability and achievement compared with the local state schools. He also had adequate school social skills. However, the emotional pressure from his mother was precipitating a behavioural crisis as Shane sought ways to offload or transfer back to her the emotional turmoil she was generating. His mother's authority was being gradually eroded and there was the threat of a slide into delinquency. She had such unrealistic expectations and aspirations for Shane which threatened to impede his progress.

Shane's programme of activities took him out of the house as much as possible, and Kirsty was offered counselling to help her 'sort things out'. This achieved a number of valuable objectives. It helped her in the process of reappraising her life and taking a more realistic view of her history and the effect it had had on her. For instance, she needed to acknowledge her own vulnerability, her tendency to make poor choices of partner, and she needed confidence in decision-making. These counselling sessions provided a vehicle for sharing parenting skills and planning a strategy for managing their relationship; in particular coming to realize that Shane should become independent and 'be ordinary'. The burden of managing her emotional needs was taken off his shoulders as much as possible.

At the same time a counsellor was provided for Shane so that he could also work through his own agenda, and this continued for about ten sessions. A volunteer mentor, Vanessa, fortuitously became available and the peer mentoring and support which Kirsty would continue to need was put in place. At this time the counselling sessions were terminated. As problems arose over other aspects of Shane's case, Vanessa acted as an intermediary, to reduce conflict.

In terms of reintegration, Shane needed little support, but Kirsty was reluctant to accept the local schools as adequate. Eventually she was persuaded to follow a two-stage strategy of starting Shane in a school as quickly as possible and then transferring him once he could show a successful track record. In the event this was exactly what happened.

Shane's problems were his mother's problems by proxy. He could cope with school but would his mother let him? For instance, without our involvement she might well have withdrawn him and wrecked his school place, leaving him without a place at any school and without the right to our services (which were ring-fenced for excluded children).

Appendix 2: Child protection issues

Child protection policy

Once you start doing outreach work, a set of concerns arises that are different from those in school. You are no longer *in loco parentis*, but workers may be entering previously uncharted territory in terms of concerns about children at risk of significant harm, and staff at risk of false accusations.

You may need a guide to the Children Act – one such is *The Children Act 1989: A Guide for the Education Service* (Open University, Milton Keynes, 1990). You will also probably benefit from reading Department of Health advice in *Protecting Children: A Guide for Social Workers Undertaking a Comprehensive Assessment* (HMSO, London, 1987).

Three simple guidelines

1. Outreach workers should ensure that they make the following statement on meeting parents or adults-in-charge for the first time:
    'I will keep everything you say strictly in confidence, and just between you and me. But if you tell me something which makes me think a child might be at risk of harm, I will talk to you about my concerns and we can decide together who we need to tell.'
    If the outreach worker is a teacher they will, of course, have already explained that they are not, for the time being, there as a teacher (see Chapter 5).

2. Workers should never try to 'investigate' concerns themselves. This is a technically difficult task which must not contravene very tight rules on untainted evidence.

3. Outreach workers need to have good judgment about propriety and safety. Some teachers believe they should never be alone with a child, although this is quite normal for care, youth, and social workers.

Different norms apply. To be too sensitive to perceived risk is as bad as not being sensitive enough. *At all times, outreach workers should ensure that nothing they do could ever be open to misinterpretation.* False allegations will not stick if the worker has a completely clear conscience.

The following statistics (with acknowledgment to Trevor Moores of Westminster SSD) may be helpful in reassuring worried parents if a child protection investigation (CPI) does arise following outreach work:

- Almost all (96 per cent) of those children who are the subject of CPIs do not leave home.

- Three out of four of those who do leave for a time return very rapidly.

- Seventy per cent of parents in one survey eventually came to see the process as helpful.

- Social work arising from CPIs generally promotes better health and living conditions, improved parenting, and enhanced physical and mental development.

Appendix 3: Resources, useful information and websites

▰▰▰ Resources and information

Readers should form their own judgments about any materials, advice or transactions entered into through the organisations mentioned here. Since circumstances and personnel change, no guarantees can be given as to their continuing qualities.

Core resources for information of all kinds

- DfEE circulars – obtainable from DfEE publications centre: 0845 6022260.

- School Inclusion Division of the DfEE: 0171 9255637 or schoolinclusion@DfEE.gov.uk.

- Joseph Rowntree Foundation: 0904 629241. The JRF *Social Research Findings* are easy-to-read short reports which are an effective way of keeping abreast with core social research.

- ACE (Advisory Centre for Education, London): 0207 3548321 gives expert advice for governors, parents and outreach workers and publishes useful easy-to-read information sheets and handbooks.

- The Register of Chartered Psychologists has lists of freelance psychologists, including those specialising in children's work; obtainable from 0116 2549468 or mailto: mail@bps.org.uk.

Alcohol problems

If alcohol figures in the problems, try National Alcohol Helpline: 0345 320202. There is also a freecall dial-and-listen number: 0500 801802. Phone Alateen: 0207 4030888 for teenage children of alcohol abusers.

Bereavement

Early bereavement often underpins problems at school. CRUSE has a national network: 0208 940 4818. The Candle Project at St Christopher's Hospice is designed with children in mind: 0208 7789252. Read Ward (1992) or Machin (1994) – see the Bibliography.

Bridging courses

These are courses provided for pupils at Key Stage 4, in colleges of further education, which generally have a more vocational slant, more work experience opportunities and (in the better ones) group work and mentoring. You will probably know if your LEA operates this as a policy, but it is possible you could buy into a neighbouring authority instead or as well. Local restrictions will apply, but these projects are proliferating at a terrific rate.

Try your LEA, and 'ask around the neighbourhood' or contact DIVERT who are developing networks nationally: 0207 379 6171. There is also First Key: 0113 2432541; and Compact Club 2000: 0121 603 2220 (another national organisation).

Brief therapy

The Brief Therapy Practice: 0207 968 0070.

Bullying

The Anti-bullying Campaign: 0207 378 1446.

Child abuse

Childline: 0800 1111 (24 hours every day of the year). In an emergency contact social services.

College-based courses

INCLUDE: 01353 650350 run locally based projects for children at Key Stage 4 and may be able to offer advice or run a programme in your area.

Counselling

Every teacher would benefit by developing counselling skills. Try the *Counselling In Action* series from Sage Publications: 0207 374 0645. Contact the British Association of Counselling: 01788 578 328 for information on counselling courses available in your locality.

Drug abuse

Try SCODA (Standing Conference on Drug Abuse): 0207 928 9500 or mailto: info@scoda.demon.co.uk. There is also the Drugs Prevention Advisory Service (Head Office in London): 0207 217 8631 or mailto: homeofficedpashq@btinternet.com.

Exclusion rates

Visit the following site: http://www.inaura.net/research, or search www.news.bbc.co.uk. Examples for 1996/97:

- Portsmouth, Hammersmith and Fulham – 0.45 per cent;
- Stockton and Rotherham – 0.05 per cent.

External funding

More than 1500 charities are listed at www.caritasdata.co.uk. Alternatively get hold of a copy of the *Charities Directory* or contact the Charities Commission.

Look for business partnerships: try the big companies. Asking for money for projects is surprisingly successful if you have a project in mind. One rule seems fairly golden, though – no-one wants to give grants to fund projects which are already being funded by statutory bodies, but if you want to set up a motorbike project, a drop-in centre or a special outward bound activity you might be lucky.

Family group conferences

The Family Rights Group (The Print House, Ashwin Street, London E8 3DL): 0207 923 2628 can probably suggest a local network who can provide advice, support and training.

Family help

The Children's Society: 0207 837 4299 can give information and advice especially on family finance problems. Parenting information is available from Family and Youth Concern: 01865 556848. Help for lone parents is available from Gingerbread: 0207 336 8183. NCH Action for Children (specialist areas abuse and disability): 0207 226 2033.

Management of change in developing schools

The best organisation is sometimes hard to find. Advice on developing local projects is available. Try the author's own website: www.inaura.net. The DfEE's circular *Social Inclusion: Pupil Support* (1999) provides contact numbers for those who want to talk to managers of on-going projects.

Mediation

NACRO (National Association for the Care and Rehabilitation of Offenders) are developing mediation services across their network. They may be able to help with advice or INSET: 0207 5826500.

Mental health

Young Minds: 0207 336 8445 is an umbrella organisation with good links to the community. Trust for the Study of Adolescence is a good information resource, with materials for developing parenting skills (including videos): 01273 693311.

Mentoring and befriending

Youth at Risk are currently developing a new programme for schools and have a track record of effective youth work. It is worth finding out whether they can offer anything in your area: 01628 481814 or mailto: neil@yaruk.co.uk.

Multicultural issues

NAFSIYAT Intercultural Therapy Centre (London): 0207 2634130 does therapeutic work for people from ethnic and cultural minorities (or contact UKCP – see below). There is also the Asian People with Disabilities Alliance: 0208 961 6773; and 'Bright Futures' (African–Caribbean resources workshops and INSET): 0208 670 1653.

Parenting and parent support

Try the following: National Parenting Development Centre (London): 0207 221 4471; National Federation of Parent/Teacher Associations: 01474 560618; The Parent Network (London NW5 2DS): 0207 485 8535; Place To Be (London SW1W 0JA): 0207 823 1225; Parentline (help for stressed parents): 01702 559900; Parent Network (developing a network of local support groups): 0207 485 8535.

Psychotherapy

The UKCP (UK Council for Psychotherapy) hold lists of psychotherapists and can provide information: 0207 436 3002.

Rational–emotive therapy

Try the *Counselling in Action* series from Sage Publications: 0207 374 0645.

Remedial academic work

Read Engelmann *et al.* (1988) for a corrective reading programme – see the Bibliography. Diagnostic tests are available from NFER/Nelson, Windsor.

Respite breaks

The Victor Brusa Memorial Fund for Children have a small fund for respite breaks and in any case can offer good advice: 0207 2865127. CARE (Christian Action Research Education, based in London but operating across the UK) have a database of suitable holiday and adventure homes for young people: 0207 2330455. They won't fund a respite break, but they may provide a break that is customised to pupil and family needs.

For funding try Children in Need: 0208 735 5057, or Boys' and Girls' Welfare Society: 0161 283 4848. Better still visit www.caritasdata.co.uk/indexchr.htm for online contact information for charities that help children.

Sexuality

Try the Family Planning Association: 0207 837 5432; or the Gay and Lesbian Switchboard (advice for families and friends as well as gay young people): 0207 837 7324.

School phobia and non-attendance

Read Blagg (1987), Galloway (1985) and/or Denney (1973) – see the Bibliography.

Self-esteem

Read Bagley (1979), Cullen (1991) and/or Bourne (1994) – see the Bibliography.

Therapy

Rational–emotive, brief, cognitive, behavioural, TA, solution-focused …Therapy usually comes via the local authority or community health services, but funding streams are increasingly available direct to schools. You can find book references quickly by going to www.bl.uk (British Library online catalogue). There is also a list of resources at www.inaura.net.

Training

SENAT provide training packages for SEN support workers: 01670 534300.

▓ Websites

Websites are less stable than publications references: it is hoped that the following are not going to disappear! Whether we like it or not this is the direction in which things are going. The net has changed since you last checked it (even if that was yesterday), so it is worth getting used to navigating from site to site. Useful code-breakers are: gov (governments); co.uk (UK profit-making company); com (international commercial); org (charity or a company not-for-profit); edu (USA-based educational establishment); ac.uk (British educational establishment). Also look out for country codes, e.g.: ie = Ireland; it = Italy; za = South Africa.

News sites

- *www.dfee.gov.uk*: Nearly everything they produce for circulation is published on the web now.

- *www.open.gov.uk*: The government's 'home page'. Home Office and social services documents can be traced from here.

- *www.staying-power.com*: A useful site for information on INSET, conferences and seminars.

- *www.telegraph.co.uk*: The *Daily Telegraph* may not be your cup of tea, but its website is one of the best news sites on the net – easily searchable for information on education (or anything else).

- *www.newsint.co.uk*: Start here to reach the *Times*, the *Sun*, the *Times Educational Supplement* and the *Times Higher Educational Supplement* (amongst others).

- *www.tes.co.uk* or go straight to the *Times Educational Supplement* website.

- *www.news.bbc.co.uk*: For news online.

Education resources

- *www.primary-networks.com*: Internet advice for primary schools.

- *www.eun.org*: European schools net.

- *www.tele-school.org*: School links UK.

- *www.studyweb.com*: Curriculum links.

- *www.bht.co.uk*: An upbeat home tutoring service.

- *www.ngfl.gov.uk*: National Grid for Learning.

- *www.becta.org.uk*: British Education and Communication Agency.

- *www.vtc.ngfl.gov.uk*: The virtual teacher agency.

- *www.schoolzone.co.uk*: Various resources links.

- *www.mda.org.uk/vlmp*: British Museums (an umbrella site).

- *www.rmplc.co.uk/eduweb*: The RM site (SMILE maths is in here somewhere).

- *www.yaruk.co.uk*: The Youth at Risk site.

- *www.bl.uk*: British Library.

- *www.learnfree.co.uk*: Free education online service.

- *www.cabinet-office.gov.uk/seu*: The government's Social Exclusion Unit.

- *www.inaura.net*: INSET and consultancy for reducing exclusion and managing change – includes pages for children and parents.

Bibliography

(Text underlined indicates its relevance)

Achenbach, C.M. (1974) *Child Behaviour Checklist*, Vermont: University of Vermont.

American Psychiatric Association (1995) *Diagnostic and Statistical Manual of Mental Disorders* (4th edn, revised), Washington, DC: APA.

Audit Commission (1996) *National Report: Misspent Youth: Young People and Crime*, London: Audit Commission.

Bagley, C., Verma, G.K., Mallick, K. and Young, L. (1979) *Personality Self-Esteem and Prejudice*, London: Saxon House.

Balcombe, J., Strange, N. and Tate, G. (1993) *Wish You Were Here: How UK and Japanese Owned Organisations Manage Attendance*, London: The Industrial Society

Beckerian, D.A. and Dennett, J.L. (1993) 'The cognitive interview technique: reviving the issues', *Applied Cognitive Psychology* **7**, 275–97.

Blagg, N. (1987) *School Phobia and its Treatment*, Beckenham: Croom Helm.

Blyth, E. and Milner, J. (1993) *Exclusion from School: Interprofessional Issues for Policy and Practice*, London: Routledge.

Booth, T., Swann, W., Masterton, M. and Potts, P. (eds) (1992) *Policies for Diversity in Education*, Routledge/OU.

Bourne, J., Bridges, L. and Searle, C. (1994) *Outcast England: How Schools Exclude Black Children*, London: Insititute of Race Relations.

Bowlby, J. (1981) *Separation (Anxiety and Anger), 1973*, London: Hogarth Press.

Bowlby, J. (1981) *Sadness and Depression, 1973*. London: Penguin.

Bracey, G.W. (1996) 'The impact of early intervention: research', *Phi Beta Kappa* **77**, 510–12.

Brand, C. (1996) 'Doing something about "g"', *Intelligence* **22**, 311–26.

Brighouse, T. (1989) *Ending Segregation in Local Schools*, London: Centre for Studies on Integration in Education.

Brodie, I. and Berridge, D. (1996) *School Exclusion: Research Themes and Issues*, Luton: Luton University Press.

Ceci, S.J. (1991) 'How much does schooling influence general intelligence and its cognitive components?: a reassessment of the evidence', *Developmental Psychology* **27**, 703–23.

Chandler, L.A. (1985) *Assessing Stress in Children*, New York: Praeger Special Studies.

Coard, B. (1991) *How the West Indian Child is Made Educationally Subnormal in the British School System* (revised edn), London: Karia Press.

Coopersmith, S. (1991) *Self-Esteem Inventory*, Palo Alto, CA: Consulting Psychologists Press.

Cornwall, J. (1995) 'Pyschology, disability and equal opportunity', *The Psychologist: Bulletin of the Psychological Society* **8**, 396–7.

Cullen, P.B., Ballard, C.G., Ing, R.P. and Mohan, R.N. (1991) 'Vulnerability, coping and crisis', *European Journal of Psychiatry* **5**, 210–15.

Cullingford, L. and Morrison, J. (1996) 'Who excludes whom? The personal experiences of excluded children', in: Blyth, E. and Milner, J. (eds) *Exclusion from School: Interprofessional Issues for Policy and Practice*, London: Routledge.

Denney, A. (1973) *Truancy and School Phobias*, London: Priory Press.

DfEE (1994) *The Code of Practice on the Identification and Assessment of Special Educational Needs*, London, HMSO.

DfEE (1999) *Social Inclusion: Pupil Support: The Secretary of State's Guidance on Pupil Attendance, Behaviour, Exclusion and Reintegration*, circular 10/99, London: HMSO.

DoH (1987) *Protecting Children: A Guide for Social Workers Undertaking a Comprehensive Assessment*, London: HMSO.

Engelmann, S., Johnson, G., Carnine, L. *et al.* (1988) *Decoding Strategies: A Corrective Reading Programme*, London: Macmillan/McGraw-Hill.

Farrington, D.P. (1996) *Understanding and Preventing Youth Crime in the United Kingdom*, Joseph Rowntree Foundation.

Faulkner, A. (1990) 'Childhood bereavement and problem behaviour', *Nursing Times* **86**, 30.

Fisher, R.P. and Geiselman, R.E. (1992) *Memory Enhancing Techniques for Investigative Interviewing*, Springfield, IL: Charles C. Thomas.

Fordham, S.M. (1987) 'Black pupils' school success as related to fictive kinship: a study in the Washington DC public school system', *Dissertation Abstracts International* **48A**, 1485.

Galloway, D. (1985) *Schools and Persistent Absentees*, London: Pergamon.

Gardner, H. (1983) *Frames of Mind: The Theory of Multiple Intelligence*, New York: Basic Books.

Gardner, H. (1995) 'Reflections on multiple intelligences: myths and messages', *Phi Delta Kappa* **77**, 200–9.

Gibson, H.B. (1968) 'Research into aspects of delinquency', in *Research Relevant to the Education of Children with Learning Handicaps*, pp. 30–6, London: College of Special Education.

Goodchild, A. and Williams, C. (1994) 'Success within failure: an assessment of a parent-led response to informal school exclusion', *British Journal of Special Education* **21**, 73–6.

Graham, J. (1988) *Schools, Disruptive Behaviour and Delinquency. A Review of Research* (Research Study 96), London: HMSO.

Grizenko, N., Sayegh, L. and Papineau, D. (1994) 'Predicting outcome in a multimodal day treatment program for children with severe behaviour problems', *Canadian Journal of Psychology* **39**, 557–62.

Hayden, C. (1994) 'Primary-age children excluded from school: a multi-agency focus for concern', *Children & Society* **8**, 257–73.

HMI (1995) *Report on Pupil Referral Units: The First Twelve Inspections*, London: OfSTED.

ILEA (1985) *School Support Programme: The Reintegration of Pupils into Mainstream Schools* (RS968/85), London: ILEA Research and Statistics Branch.

Imich, A.J. (1994) 'Exclusions from school: current trends and issues', *Educational Research* **36**, 3–11.

Isen, A.M. (1993) 'Positive affect and decision-making', in: Lewis, M. and Haviland, J. (eds) *Handbook of Emotions*, London: Guilford Press.

Jewett, C. (1982) *Helping Children Cope with Separation and Loss*, London: Batsford.

John, P. (1996) 'Damaged goods? An interpretation of excluded pupil's perceptions of schooling', in: Blyth, E. and Milner, J. (eds) *Exclusion from School: Interprofessional Issues for Policy and Practice*, London: Routledge.

Johnston, M. (1996) 'Models of disability', *The Psychologist: Bulletin of the Psychological Society* **9**, 205–10.

Joseph Rowntree Foundation (1993) *Multiagency Working on Difficult-to-Manage Estates*, York: JRF.

Joseph Rowntree Foundation (1994) *The Experience of 'Excluded' Primary Schoolchildren and their Families*, York: JRF.

Kanner, L. (1943) 'Autistic disturbances of affective contact', *Nervous Child* **2**, 217–50.

Krueger, R.A. (1994) *Focus Groups: A Practical Guide for Applied Research*, London: Sage Publications.

Lawrence J (1984) *Disruptive Children – Disruptive Schools*, London: Routledge.

Lewis, M. and Haviland, J. (1993) *Handbook of Emotions*, London: Guilford Press.

Loeber, R. and Dishion, T.J. (1984) 'Boys who fight at home and school: family conditions influencing cross-setting consistency', *Journal of Consulting and Clinical Psychology* **52**, 759–68.

Machin, L. (1994) *Looking at Loss: Bereavement Counselling Pack*, Harlow: Longman.

McCalman, J. and Patton, R.A. (1992) *Change Management*, Paul Chapman.

McLean, A. (1997) 'After the belt: school processes in low-exclusion schools', *School Organisation* **7**, 303–10.

Norwich, B. (1996) 'Special education, inclusive education, or just education for all?' Inaugural Professorial Lecture. London Institute of Education.

Novaco R.W. (1975) *Anger Control: The Development and Evaluation of an Experimental Treatment CY*, Lexington, MA: D.C. Heath/Lexington Books.

OfSTED (1993) *Education for Disaffected Pupils*, London: Office for Standards in Education.

OfSTED (1995) *The Education of Children Who are Looked After by Local Authorities*, London: Office for Standards in Education.

Open University (1990) *The Children Act 1989: A Guide for the Education Service* (pp. 6), Milton Keynes: Open University.

Parfrey, V. (1997) 'Exclusion: failed children or systems failure?' *School Organisation* **14**, 107–20.

Parsons, C (1995) Final report to the Dept. for Education on Exclusions, Canterbury, Kent: Department of Education, Canterbury Christ Church College.

Parsons, C., Castle, F., Howlett, K. and Worrall, J. (1996) Exclusion from School – the public cost. London: Commission for Racial Equality.

Parsons, C. (1999) *Education, Exclusion and Citizenship*, London, Routledge.

Phillips, A. (1993) *The Trouble with Boys*, London: HarperCollins.

Rogers, C. (1954) *Psychotherapy and Personality Change: Coordinated Studies in the Client-Centred Approach*, Chicago: University of Chicago Press.

Rutter, M., Maughan, B., Mortimore, P., Ouston, J. and Smith, A. (1979) Fifteen Thousand Hours: Secondary Schools and their Effects on Children. Cambridge, Mass.: Harvard University Press.

SEU, 1998: See websites, p. 192

Skaalvik, S. (1993) 'Ego-involvement and self-protection among slow learners: four case studies', *Scandinavian Journal of Educational Research* **37**, 305

Snyder, J. and Patterson, G. (1987) 'Family interaction and delinquent behaviour', in: Quay, H.C. (ed.) *Handbook of Juvenile Delinquency*, New York: John Wiley.

Spielberger, C. (1973) *State/Trait Anxiety Scale for Children*, Palo Alto, CA: Consulting Psychologists Press.

Stein, N.L., Trabasso, T. and Liwag, M. (1993) 'The representation and organization of emotional experience: unfolding the emotion episode', in: Lewis, M. and Haviland, J. (eds) *Handbook of Emotions*, London: Guilford Press.

Stewart, I. and Joines, V. (1991) *TA Today: A New Introduction to Transactional Analysis* (revised edn), Nottingham: Lifespace Publishing.

Still, P. and O'Keefe, D. (1989) *Officially Present*, Oxford: Institute of Economic Affairs.

Stirling, M. (1992) 'How many pupils are being excluded?' *British Journal of Special Education* **19**, 29–30.

Sutton, D. (1996) *The Essential Ingredients of Offender Programmes*, Dinas Powys: Cognitive Centre Foundation (SSD Ltd).

Topping, K. (1983) *Educational Systems for Disruptive Adolescents*, London: Croom Helm.

Ward, B. (1992) *Good Grief*, Uxbridge: J. Kingsley.

Warnock, M. for the Department of Education and Science (1978) *Report of the Committee of Enquiry into the Education of Handicapped Children and Young People*, London: HMSO.

Webb, M.H. (1995) 'Pipal Bilong Music Tru [A Truly Musical People]: musical culture, colonialism and identity in Northeastern New Britain, Papua New Guinea, after 1875', *Dissertation Abstracts International* **56A**, 1868.

Wolfelt, A. (1991) *Helping the Bereaved Child*, Fort Collins, CO: *Bereavement Magazine*/Centre for Loss and Life Transition.

Wylie, R.C. (1974) *The Self Concept*, Lincoln, NE: Nebraska Press.

Index